Introduction to Business Ownership

FOR VETERANS AND MILITARY SERVICE MEMBERS

Introduction to Business Ownership

FOR VETERANS AND MILITARY SERVICE MEMBERS

AUTHORS:

Mr. Larry Broughton,
Mr. Phil Dyer, CFP®, RLP®, CPCC
Dr. J. Michael Haynie, Ph.D.
Mr. Gary Shaheen, M.P.A.
and Mr. Mirza Tihic, M.B.A.

**Introduction to Business Ownership:
For Veterans and Military Service Members**
is a publication of the Institute for Veterans
and Military Families at Syracuse University.

"in service to those who have served"

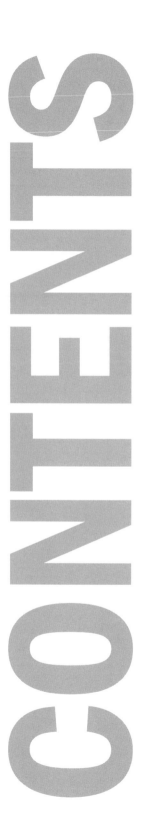

CONTENTS

Welcome

Veterans and military personnel returning from active duty are over-represented in entrepreneurship. One in seven veterans is self-employed or is a small business owner, and about one quarter of veterans are interested in starting or buying their own business.

At the U.S. Small Business Administration (SBA), one of our most important roles is supporting those men and women who have returned home from active duty and are looking to start a small business, and we offer a variety of programs and services specifically designed to do just that.

If you are a veteran who…

- Is establishing or expanding a small business, we offer a range of financing opportunities, including microloans and the Patriot Express Loan Program.

- Needs counseling, training, or one-on-one mentoring, we have Veteran Business Outreach Centers, Small Business Development Centers, Women's Business Centers and SCORE chapters to provide these services. Find the Resource Partner nearest you at *www.sba.gov/direct.*

- Is interested in competing for federal contracts, we can help you register your business, increasing your chances of success. This year we also created the Mentor-Protégé Program for Service-Disabled Veteran Owned Small Businesses to help these entrepreneurs learn how to do business with the federal government.

We also chair the Interagency Task Force on Veterans Small Business Development which improves and expands opportunities for veteran business owners.

We also offer three additional programs through our partnership with Syracuse University. The Entrepreneurship Bootcamp for Veterans with Disabilities delivers entrepreneurship training for service-disabled veterans of the wars in Iraq and Afghanistan who want to start or grow small businesses.

Operation Endure & Grow provides high quality online training, networking, and mentoring to support National Guard and Reservists and military family members.

And Veterans as Women Igniting the Spirit of Entrepreneurship delivers high quality training, networking, and mentoring in locations across the U.S. to women veterans from any branch/era of service.

Even though we have worked hard to support and assist veteran business owners, we believe we can do even more. And that is why we teamed with our Resource Partners and the Institute for Veterans and Military Families at Syracuse University to create the Operation Boots to Business program.

The leadership and management skills veterans learned during their service have positioned them become successful entrepreneurs. SBA and our partners deliver an effective introduction to entrepreneurship, educating returning service men and women about the opportunities and realities of entrepreneurship so they can plan effectively for themselves and their families. For all of those who choose to become entrepreneurs, we'll be there for them throughout the life of their businesses with the resources they need to grow, succeed, and create jobs.

With warmest regards,

Karen G. Mills
Administrator
U.S. Small Business Administration

Introduction

Entrepreneurship is commonly described as the act of pursuing the opportunity to generate economic value through the creation and cultivation of new businesses, positioned to satisfy a market-based need or demand. Entrepreneurship has been demonstrated to be important for economic development, national and individual wealth creation, productivity, and new job creation.

It is important to note that throughout history, business ownership has been a means through which military veterans have engaged the economic engine of their communities, and ultimately, our nation. Consider that prior military service is one of the strongest predicators of who in this country is likely to start a business. Military veterans represent approximately 6% of the U.S. population, while veterans account for almost 15% of all business owners.

In 1985, the Mid-Atlantic Research Company conducted a survey on behalf of the U.S. Veterans Administration and the U.S. Small Business Administration (SBA), demonstrating that historically 41.5% of those who served in the military have been self-employed, as compared to 24.5% of non-veterans. Looking to prior post-war periods, it's clear that business ownership represented a compelling vocation for transitioning service members. Nearly half, 49.7%, of World War II veterans went on to own or operate a business, as did 40% of Korean War veterans. Today, the SBA estimates that 20% of veterans are actively pursuing business ownership.

So, why are military veterans drawn in such large numbers to entrepreneurship, and why do they find such success? More specifically, as you consider your transition from military to civilian life, could business ownership be the 'right' path for you? This book was written to help transitioning service members answer such questions.

To be clear, business ownership is hard. More new businesses fail than succeed. This book was written based on the collective experiences of a group of educators and entrepreneurs who have many years of experience working with military veterans in the pursuit of business ownership. Our goal is to leverage this publication as a means to share many of those 'hard-learned' lessons, to help individuals considering business ownership as a post-military career make well-informed decisions.

I am a professor of entrepreneurship. Business ownership is what I teach, it's what I study, and it's my passion. Importantly, I'm also a military veteran. When I bring these two things together, I'm excited by the momentum in this country of supporting veteran entrepreneurship. In the end, I would suggest that if you believe that business ownership might be in your future, you are making the transition to civilian life at an exciting time. More so than at any other time in our history, today there are numerous programs and resources available to support veterans in the pursuit of business ownership. Further, there is a growing community of veteran business owners eager to assist other veterans as they realize their entrepreneurial goals and aspirations.

I'll leave you with this thought: business ownership has been described as the 'most democratic and freedom creating' of all vocations. If that's the case, who better to pursue business ownership than the men and women who understand what it means to fight for freedom and democracy? In other words, who better to 'live' the American Dream of business ownership than those who have defended that dream through military service? For me, the answers to such questions are clear, and I believe that we are on the way toward cultivating an exceedingly powerful network of veteran entrepreneurs across this country.

It is my hope that this publication helps you understand the potential of business ownership as a post-military vocation, both the good and the bad, in a way that empowers you to make informed choices about jobs, careers, and your future vocational endeavors.

Mike H

Dr. J. Michael Haynie, Ph.D.
Executive Director and Founder
Institute for Veterans and Military Families
Barnes Professor of Entrepreneurship
Martin J. Whitman School of Management
Syracuse University
U.S. Air Force Veteran

Veteran Business Owner Profile

John Raftery served in the initial invasion of Iraq as a member of a U.S. Marine Corps Force Recon Unit, the Marine Corps term for Special Forces. After being deployed for a year, John returned to his young family with impaired hearing, chronic pain in his knees and back and severe PTSD. Yet, he considers himself lucky. He says, "Many of the Marines I served with had it much worse than I did."

NAME: John Raftery

PROGRAM: Entrepreneurship Bootcamp for Veterans with Disabilities (EBV), Syracuse University, Class of 2007

BRANCH: U.S. Marine Corps

BUSINESS: Patriot Contractors

Like many veterans, John had difficulty finding work when he left the Marine Corps and returned home to his family. Eventually, John took a part time job as an accounting assistant in Dallas, Texas.

Dissatisfied with his job and his future prospects, John read about the Entrepreneurship Bootcamp for Veterans with Disabilities at Syracuse University (EBV) online. He had always wanted to start a business, and thought the EBV program might offer the fresh start he and his wife, Michelle, were looking for after the Marine Corps.

After completing the EBV program in 2007, John launched Patriot Contractors, a "finish" construction company (founded in 2008). A service-disabled, veteran-owned company, Patriot Contractors has witnessed growth in revenues and employees each and every year of operation. Today, John employs 21 individuals, and in 2010, his company generated revenues that hit $2 million. Patriot Contractors exceeded $5 million in revenues at the end of 2011.

Despite working 60 to 80 hours per week, John says, "I'm having a great time. It's very freeing."

Learn more about Patriot Contractors at *patriot1.com.*

CHAPTER 1

Business Ownership as a Bridge to Civilian Life

"One of the greatest assets that a service member brings to the civilian work world is a single-minded focus on accomplishing the mission, along with the supervisory, management, and technical skills essential for mission success."

John Raftery enlisted in the U.S. Marine Corps when he was 19. Assigned to the 1st Recon Battalion at Camp Pendleton, John deployed to Iraq as part of the initial invasion, and spent more than a year 'in country.' After his deployment, John returned to his young family with impaired hearing, chronic pain in his knees and back, and struggled with depression. Yet, he considers himself lucky. "Many of the Marines I served with had it much worse than I did," he says.

In 2006, Corporal Raftery made the decision to leave the Marine Corps, but wasn't sure what he wanted to do with the rest of his life. He knew two things for sure: he needed to pursue a post-service vocation that would support his young family and he didn't want to take orders anymore. He wanted to be his own boss. John, like many other military veterans, made the decision that his best path to professional and personal satisfaction after military service was to pursue business ownership.

In 2007, John launched Patriot Contractors, a commercial construction company. Today, after years of commitment and hard work, he is a successful business owner. What started out as a company of two employees (John and his wife, Michelle), is today a firm that employs more than 25 full-time employees, many of whom are veterans. Last year, the company generated more than $5 million in revenues. Despite working more than 60 hours a week, John says, "I'm having a great time. Business ownership is very freeing."

John's story is extraordinary, but not unusual for military veterans. In fact, prior military service is one of the strongest predicators of who is most likely to start a business in the U.S. In other words, if you served in the military, you are much more likely, as compared to those who did not serve, to launch and grow a business. Why? It's a good question and one that this guide is intended to answer.

Specifically, the purpose of this guide is to help provide insight into business ownership as a vocational strategy for service members making the transition from military to civilian life. Importantly, the goal of this guide is not to convince you to pursue business ownership as a post-service vocation. Business ownership is hard, and honestly, most new businesses fail within the first five years. Entrepreneurship is not for everyone. But, it is the right choice for some people. This guide is intended to provide you with the information you need to decide if business ownership is the right path for you!

Importantly, our purpose with this guide is not to teach you how to start a business, but to instead help you become educated as to the steps, stages, and activities associated with launching and growing a business and how the choice to pursue business ownership might align (or not) with your own personal strengths and life goals. At the end of the day, the choice is always **yours**!

It is our hope and only goal that this guide is positioned to help you make a choice that is well-informed, and in the best interest of you and your family.

What is Entrepreneurship?

Ask any 10 people what it means to be an entrepreneur and you're likely to get 10 different answers. According to textbooks, entrepreneurship is "the pursuit of opportunity without regard for resources." This is a fancy way of saying that entrepreneurship is about recognizing an opportunity to launch and grow a business, sometimes having to beg and borrow the money required to get the business off the ground.

What this ultimately means is that entrepreneurship is about *action*. What makes entrepreneurs different from others is that they are motivated. They recognize an opportunity to create a product or service that has value in the marketplace and **act** on that opportunity.

Essentially, entrepreneurial action is about recognizing an opportunity to create a product or service that is valued in the market place; enough so that it can sustain an ongoing venture. It's important to note that this is a different idea than simply recognizing an opportunity to create a product that you can sell. Instead, we're talking about an opportunity to create a product or service offering that has enough value in the marketplace to support the creation of a business structure that will be viable over the long-term. (We'll cover more on this topic in Chapter 4.)

There are many different paths to entrepreneurial action. You can start a new business from scratch, you can buy an existing business, you can launch a franchise, or you can join a family business that you ultimately take over and manage. (Again, we'll talk in more detail about each of these paths to business ownership in Chapter 3 of this guide.) However, in all cases the basic fundamentals of business ownership are the same. Whether we're talking about a family business or a franchise, or a for-profit versus a not-for-profit business, you'll need to understand markets and industries, basic accounting systems, product design and development, etc. These are, however, topics for another day and more advanced training. Rather than focus on the "nuts and bolts" of business ownership now, we'll instead focus our attention on helping you understand how to answer the question if business ownership is right for you.

"Is business ownership 'right' for me?"

On TV and in magazines, you'll read about people describing an "entrepreneurial personality"—that it takes a special type of person to be a successful entrepreneur. The reality is, that's not necessarily true and not supported by academic research. Whether you're shy or outgoing, have a college degree, or not, are a man or a woman, or come from a family background in business ownership, or not, all types of people

can be successful business owners. That being said, we **do** know a few things that successful entrepreneurs have in common.

- **PASSION:** Successful entrepreneurs exhibit a passion for both launching and growing their business, and also for the product or service they are selling.

- **TENACITY AND PERSEVERANCE:** Entrepreneurship is hard, and there will be many setbacks along the way. Successful business owners press ahead, learning from failures.

- **RESILIENCY:** Related to the above, successful entrepreneurs look forward—not back. Failure is going to happen, and the ability of the business owner to recover emotionally from small failures along the entrepreneurial journey is critical.

- **LEADERSHIP:** Successful entrepreneurs are leaders. They have the ability to craft a powerful vision for what they want to create, and then garner the support of others.

Do any of these attributes sound familiar? Do you bring these attributes to your personal approach to work and life? If the answer is yes, that's a first sign that business ownership might be in your future. However, this is only a small piece of a complicated decision-making process. It's also important to understand what the entrepreneurial lifestyle is all about, and what it might mean for you and your family.

Four Myths About Entrepreneurs

1 **Entrepreneurs are born, not made.**
There is no research to support the notion that entrepreneurs are born, or that they are a special personality type. No one is born to be an entrepreneur; everyone has the potential to become one.

2 **Entrepreneurs are gamblers.**
The truth is, entrepreneurs are usually moderate risk takers, as are most people.

3 **Entrepreneurs are motivated primarily by money.**
Money is important, but research suggests that it is not the primary reason that entrepreneurs start new firms.

4 **Entrepreneurs should be young and energetic**
The average entrepreneur in the U.S. is between 35 and 45 years-old and has 10 or more years of experience in a large organization.

Entrepreneurship as a Vocation

One of the greatest misconceptions about business ownership is that it's "easier" than a traditional job, that you'll have more free time and work less hours. **Nothing** could be further from the truth. As a small business owner, you **are** the business—24/7.

Typically, we hear from successful entrepreneurs that they work 50-80 hours per week on their businesses. Juggling work and personal life can be a daunting challenge. As an entrepreneur, you probably find yourself fighting each day to balance your daily life with customers, marketing, employees, and business development, let alone family, friends, and personal pursuits. Even

YOU ARE THE BUSINESS 24/7

among the most savvy and driven business owners, there is a tendency to focus too much on the business tasks at hand, leaving critical personal affairs unattended. So, why pursue business ownership? Every coin has two sides, and the vocation of entrepreneurship also offers some compelling up-sides for those willing to work hard and persevere. Here are a few of the most common motivations for pursuing business ownership expressed by entrepreneurs.

Common motivations for pursuing business ownership expressed by entrepreneurs:

- **AUTONOMY AND CONTROL:** Business ownership is a means through which individuals can assume a strong sense of autonomy and control over their lives. As a business owner, you answer to yourself and your customers. The choices you make (good or bad) in regard to the product and service you offer, markets you enter, and even when you come to work, are yours alone.

- **PURSUIT OF INDIVIDUAL IDEAS AND INITIATIVE:** Business ownership represents a means through which you can express your own individuality, by the pursuit of ideas that are important to you.

- **LIFESTYLE:** Related to the first motivation above, business ownership represents a means to balance work and life in a way that is your own.

- **FINANCIAL REWARD:** Business ownership is a high-risk vocation, but the potential for reward is also high. No entrepreneur should start a business only motivated by the desire to "get rich." If you're passionate about your business and the value inherent in the product or service you are selling, you will very likely realize a positive financial reward.

So, business ownership is hard and it requires passion, commitment, and resiliency. Doesn't this sound like what they tell you it takes to be successful in the military? Doesn't this sound like what they teach you in the military?

It shouldn't be any surprise that military veterans have long been drawn to business ownership as a post-service vocation.

Veteran Business Ownership in the U.S.

Veteran business ownership has a long and proud tradition in the U.S. Nearly half (49.7%) of World War II veterans owned and operated a business after leaving military service, and 40.1% of Korean War veterans became entrepreneurs.

Data released in May 2011 by the U.S. Census Bureau showed that today more than 2.4 million veterans are business owners, which accounts for close to 10% of all businesses nationwide. Veteran-owned businesses generated $1.2 trillion in receipts last year and employed nearly 5.8 million people. If we include businesses where veterans co-own the business with a non-veteran, the role of veteran business ownership in the U.S. is even more impactful. Businesses in which veterans were part-owners (with a non-veteran) number 3.7 million, representing 13.5% of all businesses nationwide and accounting for more than $1.6 trillion in annual receipts. These 3.7 million businesses employed 8.2 million people. Nearly one-third of veteran-owned businesses are operated in the professional, scientific, technical services, and construction sectors.

The U.S. Small Business Administration (SBA) estimates that currently 20% of veterans are actively looking to start, purchase, or partner in small business start-up. This trend of business ownership has historic roots and implies that military experience provides veterans with unique qualities and attitudes that suit the entrepreneurial process. These numbers also suggest that military experience is well-aligned with the commitment, diligence, and persistence essential to success as a business owner. This argument is also supported by a study released by the SBA's Office of Advocacy which indicates that more than one-third of both new veteran entrepreneurs (and current veteran business owners) had gained skills from their active duty service that were directly relevant to business ownership. Furthermore, in the same study 36.4% of new veteran entrepreneurs indicated that they made use of one or more technologies while on active duty service that were of "direct relevance to the operation" of their new business enterprise or self-employment activity. In addition, 32% of new veteran entrepreneurs had classes while on active duty (other than to learn the use of new technologies) that would be "of direct relevance to the operation" of their new business enterprise or self-employment activity. Interestingly, 52% of service-disabled veterans benefited from technological training during active duty that was later of use in their business. Hence, in addition to managerial skills, the study suggests that veterans gain technical skills applicable to their entrepreneurial pursuits.

As indicated above, there seems to be a natural and powerful linkage between success as a business owner and the knowledge, skills, and abilities learned through military service. Importantly, you must also remember that in most cases the decision to pursue business ownership will potentially impact not only you, but those around you. One of the greatest myths about business ownership is the notion of the entrepreneur as the lone wolf, forging ahead alone in pursuit of his or her entrepreneurial dreams. The reality is: nothing is further from the truth.

Person- and Family-Centered Business Planning

Talk to any successful business owner, and they'll tell you that it was a team effort. More than that, they'll talk first about how important it was that they had the support of their family and friends throughout the process of launching and growing their venture.

It is important to recognize that in order for you to find success as a business owner, there must be a fit between your personal strengths and your business idea. It's equally important to recognize that your success or failure as a business owner will also be determined in large part by your approach to planning your business in a way that also complements (and leverages) the support of your friends and family.

One of the great advantages of business ownership is the opportunity to build a business that affords the flexibility to remain engaged with family activities. However, business ownership has an insidious tendency to become all-consuming, sometimes in a way that results in the business owner neglecting obligations to family and friends. In the end, this situation has negative consequences for the entrepreneur, the business, and the family. As you consider the possibility of business ownership as a transition strategy from military to civilian life, it is critical that you seek the input and support of those individuals that will ultimately represent your personal support system throughout your entrepreneurial journey. Identify those individuals right now, and consider involving them in your decision-making and business planning process. Doing so will help you understand their strengths and how they might represent valuable resources in the context

> "One of the great advantages of business ownership is the opportunity to build a business that affords the flexibility to remain engaged with family activities."

of supporting your growing venture. A proactive discussion with family members will also help you understand their fears and concerns in the context of your decision to forgo the "traditional" 9-5 job, and the steady paycheck that comes with it.

As you are engaging with family and friends to help you arrive at a decision as to whether or not business ownership is "right" for you and your family, **we recommend you approach those conversations with the following in mind**:

TIP 1: Be upfront and honest about both the opportunity (as you see it) and the potential risks.

TIP 2: Take time to really understand the point of view of others—and really listen!

TIP 3: Understand that this process is an ongoing dialogue—it is not about arriving at a consensus decision after the first conversation.

TIP 4: Have a frank discussion about what you expect in regard to the role that family members might play in the business. Also, be open to a discussion about what the family expects from you in regard to balancing your commitments to family, and the business.

TIP 5: Seek more information and insights from those with whom you disagree. Ask for more detail and examples that will enable you to better understand other points of view.

TIP 6: While disagreements on issues may be strong, don't forget that family values are a shared bond and represent a shared commitment to ultimately what is in the best interest of the family.

TIP 7: Create "rules of behavior" for family meetings and abide by them. That means you, too!

TIP 8: Set priorities appropriately! Businesses are created for many reasons—to earn lots of money, or even to change the world. That said, it is important to prioritize family relationships over business. At the end of the day, you can build another business or make more money, but you've only got one family for life. Remembering that can help put disagreements into perspective.

One of the greatest assets that a service member brings to the civilian work world is a single-minded focus on accomplishing the mission, along with the supervisory, management, and technical skills essential for mission success. In the next chapter, we will discuss how and why your experience in the military is uniquely positioned to support the successful pursuit of business ownership.

Veteran Business Owner Profile

NAME: Larry Broughton

HOMETOWN: Orange County, Calif.

BRANCH: U.S. Army

BUSINESS: Broughton Hospitality

Larry Broughton is an award-winning entrepreneur, best-selling author and keynote speaker. After growing up in a small mill town in rural New York, he spent nearly eight years with the U.S. Army's elite Special Forces, commonly known as the Green Berets. Larry has parlayed his unique experience of serving on Special Forces teams to the business world.

He is founder, president and CEO of Broughton Hospitality. Since its inception, his firm has received numerous awards for performance, and is considered a leader in the boutique hotel industry. He has been awarded Ernst & Young's prestigious Entrepreneur of the Year Award®; the National Veteran-Owned Business Association named him their Vetrepreneur of the Year; he has been awarded Coastline College District's Visionary of the Year, while Entrepreneur magazine named his firm among their Hot 500 Fastest Growing Privately Held Companies

Because of his belief in the power of entrepreneurship, Larry devotes a great deal of his time coaching and mentoring current and aspiring entrepreneurs toward success. His upbeat, creative approach to business has been featured in articles from the *Los Angeles Times* and *New York Times* to *Entrepreneur* magazine; on dozens of national radio shows; on every major television network; and he has made multiple appearances on CNBC's *The Big Idea* with Donny Deutsch.

Larry is the co-author of "The Next Big Thing: Top Trends to Dominate the New Economy" (Celebrity Press, 2011), as well as "VICTORY: 7 Entrepreneur Success Strategies for Veterans" (Bandera Publishing, 2011). He is also the author of the upcoming books "FLASHPOINTS For Achievers," as well as "Green Beret Lessons on Leadership."

He lives in Orange County, Calif., with his bride, Suzanne; their daughter, Emily; and son, Ben.

Learn more at *LarryBroughton.net*, *BroughtonHospitality.com,* and *VictorySuccessSystem.com.*

CHAPTER 2

Relating Military Skills and Service to Business Ownership

> "Entrepreneurs and business owners are the warriors of today's business world."

Take a moment to reflect on your military experience—whether three years or 30—and about those with whom you served. What are some of the words and phrases that immediately come to mind?

Discipline. Tenacity. Dedication to mission. Selflessness. Improvise, adapt, and overcome. "Never-Say-Die" attitude. Sacrifice. Motivation. Teamwork. Bold. Real world leadership. Inspirational. Unshakable belief in a higher purpose. Risk-taker. Initiative. Determination.

Sound about right?

These are qualities, values, and mindset attributes that differentiate those that raise their hand, take the oath, and write that blank check to Uncle Sam, from the general population. What's more, every single word and phrase above is **also** used to describe those that step up and take on the challenges—and rewards—of entrepreneurship.

Entrepreneurs and business owners are the warriors of today's business world. They are the innovators, the visionaries, the trailblazers, and the risk-takers who are ready, willing, and able to step away from the relative security of an ordinary job, take on the uncertainty of business ownership, and create something extraordinary for themselves, their families, their employees, and their community.

Do you have "the right stuff" to take on business ownership and become a military veteran entrepreneur (MVE)? If so, you will be in great company! MVEs just like you started every one of these household names:

NIKE	FEDEX	GODADDY	CHICK-FIL-A
Phil Knight	Fred Smith	Bob Parsons	S. Truett Cathy
U.S. Army	*U.S. Marine Corps*	*U.S. Marine Corps*	*U.S. Army*
LITTLE CAESARS PIZZA	MAIL BOXES ETC. THE UPS STORE	PEROT SYSTEMS	AMERICA ONLINE/AOL
Michael Ilitch	Jim Amos	Ross Perot	James Kimsey
U.S. Marine Corps	*U.S. Marine Corps*	*U.S. Navy*	*U.S. Army*

While these MVE-founded companies employ tens of thousands and have worldwide reach, far more have even more significant local impact. There are currently around 3 million veteran-owned business nationally (approximately 14% of all small businesses), with one in seven veterans electing entrepreneurship.

One common misconception about MVEs is that they all work in government or defense contracting. The truth? Over 80% of veteran-owned businesses are outside of these areas. From web design to limousine services, from organic farms to graphic artists and personal security companies, the opportunities are virtually limitless.

There is no doubt about it...veterans make **great** entrepreneurs! We strongly encourage you to explore business ownership as a viable option as you transition from military service.

In the rest of this chapter, we will connect key entrepreneur success strategies distilled from hundreds of interviews with top entrepreneurs, CEOs and business owners and share how you can leverage your military experience and values to turn these strategies into business success.

This will help you begin to formulate your customized "battle plan" of specific strategies you can apply to any potential business; from a one-person operation or small ensemble firm to a national (or international) multi-site company being built for eventual sale or to go public.

As you read, brainstorm how these strategies might help you—the aspiring MVE—achieve financial success with your business, and empower you to create an organization that is a reflection of your individual passion, brilliance, unique skills, and core values. These strategies are, quite literally, your keys to entrepreneurial **VICTORY**:

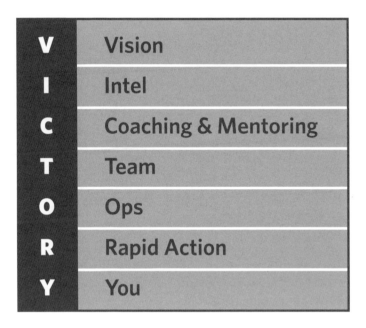

V	Vision
I	Intel
C	Coaching & Mentoring
T	Team
O	Ops
R	Rapid Action
Y	You

Strategy 1: Vision

Vision is very similar to the mission of a military operation—a clear idea of what the ultimate goal is and what the benefits of accomplishing the mission will be. However, while a military mission statement is second nature to most transitioning service members, many aspiring MVEs lack a clear vision of what they are **truly** capable of achieving.

They don't yet realize the positive impact a successful business can have on their families, clients/customers, and broader communities. The reason? They haven't connected with their own unique strengths and abilities, their core values, and their guiding principles (the very things that form the foundation of sustainable success) to craft a guiding vision for both personal and business success.

If you want to build an exceptional organization, one that moves from good to great, you MUST have a clearly stated vision to guide you. Experience shows that the vast majority of wildly successful organizations share several common characteristics. Chief among them is a clear vision of where they're going and what success means for them. In fact, there's no more important strategy to attain enduring success than vision. Long-term, sustainable success will evade you, unless you possess a clear vision of where you're going as an organization, and as a person.

Why is vision so important?

Vision allows you as a leader to effectively communicate your ideas, goals, and aspirations. We're not just talking about physical, tangible goals. It also includes your core values—those foundational principles in your life that guide everything you do. Vision keeps you going in the right direction, even when you are facing the trials and tribulations that entrepreneurs go through at every level of business.

> "People want and need something to aspire to—they want to be part of something greater than themselves."

As an aspiring MVE, you're like an early explorer. You must have a vision of what lies just beyond the horizon, and what the future can hold. A clear vision becomes your battle cry, your call to action. This kind of vision attracts top performers who become great team members and inspires them to give their best. It ignites creativity. It also helps us connect with the customers that are going to be most loyal to our company: the ones that will become raving fans.

Remember, we're talking about creating a vision for your business. We find that many aspiring MVEs have a clear personal vision for their lives, but they haven't developed a clear vision for their businesses. Even though your personal values and core beliefs will be a big part of your company, you still need a company vision that attracts and motivates your team members, and propels your business to a new level.

Your vision doesn't need to be complicated or earth shattering. In fact, the simpler and more realistic it is, the more compelling it can be—although, it should be one that stretches and inspires your company to great heights. If you develop a vision that is too idealistic or overly optimistic, it is guaranteed that your team members will become frustrated. Be certain it's a vision that people will be proud to be part of, either as a team member or as a customer.

People want and need something to aspire to—they want to be part of something greater than themselves. When you present your team members with a vision of the great things that the team can accomplish together, you give them a chance to be part of something bigger. This will be especially attractive to high achievers who love to be challenged.

Now you may be thinking, "This all sounds great, but how the heck do I do it?"

Here are a few examples of leading company vision statements to get you thinking:

- **APPLE:** Apple is committed to bringing the best personal computing experience to students, educators, creative professionals, and consumers around the world through its innovative hardware, software, and internet offerings.

- **GOOGLE:** To develop a perfect search engine.

- **FEDEX:** Our absolutely, positively spirit puts our customers at the heart of everything we do.

- **PERFECT FITNESS** (founded by former Navy SEAL Alden Mills): Creating solutions to allow consumers of all fitness levels to unlock their body's potential.

Hopefully, the vision statements above can get your creative juices flowing and start connecting you with the positive impact possible through entrepreneurship.

Key **Vision** Concepts

✔ Vision is critical for creating enduring success.

✔ Vision keeps you on course when business gets tough.

✔ Vision helps attract and retain the right team.

Strategy 2: Intel

A surefire way to lose on the battlefield is to charge ahead without enough intelligence to make informed decisions. The same thing is true in business. Too many MVEs launch their business with incomplete intel on key areas that are essential for short- and long-term success.

Most importantly, many of them lack understanding of their most important assets: their own strengths and weaknesses! Think of all of the battles, campaigns, and wars that have been lost due to faulty intelligence or by leaders ignoring the good intel they were given. History is replete with such examples (Cannae, Custer, McClellan, D-Day, Pearl Harbor—and the list goes on).

As military service members, we understand that intel is a key success component of any campaign. We must have an adequate understanding of key facts—about our own unit, the enemy's location, their strengths, and movement. We must grasp what is going on around us in order to reach our objective and complete our mission. The same principle applies in business. If you are going to lead a company to the place you envision, you **must** have the right intel. Let's make sure that we are clear on this: you cannot lead a successful organization without proper intelligence!

The first thing that you must understand about gathering intelligence is that we're not talking about black ops, or CIA-type skullduggery. In the business context, intel means possessing intimate knowledge of our product or service and the desires of our anticipated consumer; gathering information about market and industry conditions; and key information about our own capabilities and that our competitors. Sorry, but it's not always sexy, fun, or exciting—which is exactly why many MVEs don't like to do it!

The whole idea of sitting down and doing research, connecting with the resources we need, or just finding out what those resources are, can be a challenge and major energy drain for many MVEs. But, the rewards for making the commitment to the sometimes tedious work of gathering intel, in effect doing what many of your potential competitors won't, are well worth it.

Since intel is so vital to your success, we'll explore more fully how to gather it and what to do with the information once you get it. The good news? We're living in the best time ever to obtain solid intel on your competition and target industry. It's never been easier (or cheaper) to get the information you need to explore whether your business idea is viable, what tools you need to develop and market your business, how you can build virtual teams to drastically lower on-going business costs, and how you can directly connect with your ideal client or customer.

The ability to know whether your idea can be successful is really at the heart of gathering intel. If you find out that there is a place for your idea—that people want it, and you can carve out a spot for yourself in the market—it gives you the confidence to drive on. If you find out that your idea may not work in its current context, then you have the information you need to rethink your approach, or move on to another idea altogether. No matter what you discover, intel is a critical first step in achieving success. So, what are the best approaches to gathering the intel you need?

In its simplest form, **intel includes three things**:

1 gathering information;

2 processing and analyzing that information; and

3 disseminating and acting on the information.

> "To lack intelligence is to enter the ring blindfolded"
>
> - General David M. Shoup
> U.S. Marine Corps

Of course, the first part—gathering—is easier to do if you're working in a field where you have significant experience and contacts. In this case, connect with and leverage your own experiences, current associates or colleagues, former colleagues, former bosses and managers, and your industry contacts.

If you're a neophyte to an industry, it's more of a challenge. Where do you begin? Start by getting the big picture. This macro perspective will help you see the broad outline of your industry and gain answers to key questions, such as: (1) How large is the market? (2) What are the developing trends? (3) Who are the major players? (4) What are the opportunities and pitfalls?

Every industry has at least one trade or professional association, and these are great sources of initial information. These associations exist to provide people with facts and statistics about their industry, provide continuing education, and connect the industry with their clients/customers and suppliers. Once you get the big picture and really understand the industry, start painting a detailed picture of your own business.

Want to shorten your learning curve and gain a deeper perspective in a short amount of time? Look for industry news reports; speeches given by key industry thought leaders; the presentation program or agenda for industry meetings or trade shows; and anything else that provides a clear sight picture on what's hot. Seek out and connect with industry leaders—those who are having articles written about them, receiving awards for innovation, and challenging the status quo. Study them and find out what they're doing and how. Reach out and request an informational meeting to find out where they think the industry is headed.

Don't be intimidated to ask for an information meeting. Most people love being in the role of a mentor or guru and enjoying assisting new entrants into an industry—new blood keeps industry healthy. Just remember to be respectful of that person's time and energy, and to give back as often as you can. Strive to build mutually beneficial relationships with leaders in your industry—you can only do that if you are willing to give, as well as receive, help.

A critically important intel area that many smart, dedicated MVEs overlook involves discovering whether your clients or customers actually want your product or service! This may sound absurdly simple, but if nobody wants your product (even if they need it), they won't buy it. You'd be shocked at the number of times we've had entrepreneurs tell us that they know exactly what customers need, and how they're going to educate customers to change their perception and make a fortune. Following this path, never confirming that you're offering something people want and will pay for, is a quick ticket to the poor house.

> Does your customer **want** your product or service?

Intel gathering is not easy or exciting, but it is absolutely necessary. Keep this in mind, however: the best intel is worthless if it isn't used properly.

Just gathering intel isn't enough. We must take the time to analyze and understand the information, and then develop a course of action based on level-headed analysis. A surefire recipe for business disaster is to attempt to analyze all the data ourselves. There's an old proverb: "plans go wrong for lack of advice; many advisers bring success."

This is one of the values of developing relationships with people who have been in the trenches longer than ourselves—those industry leaders we spoke of earlier. They often see things we miss, either because we don't yet have the experience or because we are so focused on our own "brilliant" idea that we don't see clearly or see the bigger picture. The saying "none of us is as smart as all of us" is very true in business. So, gather people you trust around you and enlist them to help you analyze and make sense of the intel with you.

> **Inaction** is far worse than **failure** for an entrepreneur.

For many MVEs, gathering intel isn't the problem (although it is tedious work). Analyzing the data isn't even that difficult. The hardest part is taking action on what we learn. We're convinced that the ability to take action is one of the key success factors that separate exceptional entrepreneurs from mediocre ones (see Strategy 6: Rapid Action for more information).

In order for intel to be useful, it must be acted upon. Relevant pieces of information must be disseminated to the people who need it, such as team members, investors, and key advisors. As the leader, visionary, and driver for your company, you are ultimately responsible for getting the right information into the right hands, providing strategic direction, and then acting on what you discover.

During the first Gulf War, General Norman Schwarzkopf and his staff used the intel at his disposal to develop the "Big Left Hook." The plan? Flank and bypass the bulk of the entrenched Iraqi forces, roll up their flank, engage, and destroy their "elite" Republican Guard divisions, cutting their supply lines. The Iraqis were so thoroughly defeated that the war was effectively over in 96 hours. The Allies used their intel and analysis to take massive, decisive action!

Inaction is far worse than failure for an entrepreneur. Once you've taken action, you may realize you've taken a wrong turn. What should you do? Drive on! Take course corrective action along the way. Chances are you're now smarter and wiser than before you started, just don't make the same mistake twice. Further, don't beat yourself up over the mistakes you make! Finally, whatever you do, don't listen to the naysayers who ask, "Why don't you just get a real job?" or otherwise try to tear you down.

All entrepreneurs want their businesses to get off the ground smoothly. For some, the first time they hit resistance, or when they realize they are heading down the wrong road, they become paralyzed. Sometimes the paralysis results in the inability to take another decisive action step after making a big mistake. Other times, fear comes as a result of running into some resistance; maybe from friends, family, industry experts, or even competitors. They recoil from the pushback and sit there with their engine idling, going nowhere. Don't let this happen to you!

Every entrepreneur will have failures (trust us, we know from intimate, first-hand experience). Founding Father Benjamin Franklin put it this way: "Success is moving from failure to failure without losing your enthusiasm." It is crucial that you understand this concept.

Here's a fact: every entrepreneur has missteps and makes mistakes. The way we recover from a mistake or setback makes all the difference between ultimate failure and enduring success. Our advice? When you realize you've made a mistake, reassess immediately, check your map, and get back to the right road. Don't allow fear, embarrassment, or anything else keep you from taking immediate course corrective action and forging ahead.

Key Intel Concepts

✓ Intel isn't fun or exciting, just crucial to success.

✓ Don't try to sell people a product or service you think they need, they must also **want** it!

✓ Develop intel by cultivating relationships with industry experts.

Strategy 3: Coaching & Mentoring

Coaching and mentoring is a key component of successful military service. From bootcamp onward, junior officers and enlisted personnel are trained and guided by more experienced senior officers and non-commissioned officers. Unfortunately, many aspiring MVEs forget this lesson when they launch their businesses.

The result? They are too close to their own situation to make critical decisions with any level of objectivity. In addition, they sometimes lack the experience, the network, and the resources that make all the difference between creating enduring success and suffering eternal mediocrity.

Too many MVEs buy into the myth and romance—perpetuated by popular media—of the "lone wolf" entrepreneur. Buying into this "go it alone" fable on your entrepreneurial journey is very dangerous to both your short- and long-term success. Falling prey to the lone wolf storyline also virtually guarantees you will struggle harder, waste more time and money, and take longer to achieve that success (if you make it at all).

Are there occasional lone wolf success stories? Sure.

However, objective analysis of their arduous path to eventual success often reflects decisions made from stubbornness and pride rather than clear strategic vision, determination, and true grit. The truth? Every world-class athlete, entertainer, and entrepreneur has coaches and mentors. Pause for a moment and reflect on this. How many true top performers are you aware of that reached the pinnacle of success as a lone wolf?

The lone wolf entrepreneur is one of the most destructive myths that MVEs run into on a constant basis. This myth is a staple in popular media: TV shows, movies, and even some business magazines and business-related shows perpetuate this idea that most entrepreneurs become successful on their own. They pull themselves up by their bootstraps—they didn't need any help to succeed.

The bottom line? This entrepreneurial gig is tough enough without hamstringing yourself by falling for the lone wolf myth and trying to figure all of this out on your own!

These critical success multipliers go by different names, such as coach, mentor, teacher, or advisor. You might develop a formal mentor-mentee relationship, or your coach may just be someone you call when you need a fresh set of eyes on a problem. The actual title and form of the relationship isn't really that important.

The point is that you need a trusted advisor, someone farther down the road than you are, to help you reach the highest levels of success in the shortest time possible. MVEs sometimes have trouble asking for help because we are a self-reliant bunch. We believe we should be able to figure everything out on our own and make it all work without anyone's help. We pick up this attitude because we can take care of many things on our own. Unfortunately, sometimes this translates into us thinking, "Don't ask for help, it's a sign of weakness," which, of course, couldn't be further from the truth.

The truth is we have coaches and mentors throughout our military careers. We called them by different names, such as drill instructor, team leader, platoon leader, or company commander; but these folks were coaches and mentors.

Seeing the big picture clearly is often very difficult for entrepreneurs. We are so close to our businesses, heads down and working frantically to make deadlines or get proposals, completed projects, or finished products out the door, that we can't accurately or objectively judge what's transpiring. We may miss opportunities that are literally right in front of us, overlook a critical systems flaw that can completely derail us, or simply be operating on four cylinders instead of eight. The right coach or mentor can help us step back, take in the bigger picture, and give us the perspective that we must have for sustained success.

There are a number of ways in which the right coach helps you achieve a high level of enduring success, including:

- Offering an objective external view

- Challenging preconceived notions

- Evaluating failures

- Truth-telling

- Cheerleading

The coach is there to celebrate your successes. It's always great to get a pat on the back, especially from someone else who also enjoys a significant level of success. More importantly, the coach helps you objectively evaluate your "secret success sauce" so you can see how you achieved it and learn to repeat it!

Entrepreneurship can be a lonely endeavor, especially since well-meaning spouses, family members, and friends, who simply don't get the entrepreneurial mindset, can easily tear you down without even realizing it. The simple fact that the coach is a kindred spirit who intimately understands the entrepreneurial journey is hugely important when you hit the inevitable rough patch.

Many MVEs intellectually understand that a coach is just as necessary in business as trainers, mentors, and advisors were during their time in the military. Unfortunately, many stop there and don't take making the connection with the right coach or mentor past an intellectual exercise

The right coach is like a super-strength bottle of window cleaner. Sometimes, being in business feels like you're trying to drive down a narrow highway at 90 miles per hour with fogged-up, dirty windows and a 1,000-foot drop off either side of the road. One false move and you are headed for disaster! A good coach will help you wipe away the grime and gain crystal clarity. They help you zero in on specific targets, internalize lessons from your successes and failures and help you map out the most direct route to your objective.

You want someone who will challenge you to step up, break through the visible and invisible barriers keeping you stuck and push through powerfully to the next level! Top business coaches and mentors have vast reservoirs of experience, information, and connections. They carry toolboxes filled with a variety of strategies to support you in making the leap from where you are to where you want to be. These coaches have expansive networks and will leverage those networks to connect you with other key experts, possible clients and customers, and strategic partners.

This type of coach is incredibly valuable and should be viewed as an investment, not an expense. A good coach can easily return five, 10, or even 20-fold your investment in them in short order. Just ask yourself this question, "What's the lifetime value of one good idea?"

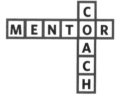

Finally, consider the financial burden and time suck being stuck in neutral; not being able to grow your business or connect with the right clients; and the difficulty attracting key team members or hiring the right staff.

Key Coaching and Mentoring Concepts

✓ All top performers in business and life use coaches/mentors.

✓ Coaches bring a critical outside perspective to your business.

✓ Coaches help you drastically reduce your learning curve.

Strategy 4: Team

Too many aspiring MVEs buy into the lone wolf myth of successful entrepreneurship. They try to do too many things themselves and never build an effective team. No organization will create enduring success without a highly effective team. To be blunt, you will never create the business you envision, the life you desire or create the positive impact you are capable of without the right team in place.

When we first mention "building a team," many aspiring MVEs break into a cold sweat as visions of payroll taxes, micromanagement headaches and "herding cats" flash before them. The truth? Teams come in many forms, from 100% virtual teams that you pay as independent contractors to the traditional multi-location organization structure with hundreds, thousands or tens of thousands of team members. The principles of team building we share in this chapter are universal, no matter what the size or complexity of the business.

Please take note that we used the term "team member" instead of "employee." We believe that "team member" is far more positive than "employee" and better reflects the rapidly changing business dynamics. Being a team member is all about shared vision and empowerment as opposed to servant vs. overseer relationships.

The most important, and most frequently overlooked, element in building a good team is you knowing yourself first. We'll explore this further later, but try to avoid the common mistake of hiring people who are just like you. Hire people who complement you, cover gaps in your know edge or experience, provide foundational support for your weaknesses and allow you to fully focus on your strengths.

Let's face it…it's hard for many of us to admit that we aren't great at everything. We're often taught to spend inordinate amounts of time trying to "fix" our perceived weaknesses instead of focusing on our extraordinary strengths. The truth is that you are not good at everything. Heck, you might not be good at most things!

That said we believe that you possess a unique combination of three to five core abilities where you are simply brilliant. These are your strengths, the areas you should focus on with laser-like intensity while outsourcing, delegating or deleting everything else to your custom-built team.

We find there are three common misconceptions that prevent MVEs from starting or expanding their team, even when they **know** they need to do so.

They are:

1. It takes too long to train someone.

2. It's quicker and easier to do things yourself.

3. It's too expensive to hire a team.

The last misconception gets to the heart of the problem. Too many entrepreneurs see hiring team members, coaches, or anything else that doesn't physically and immediately put dollars into their bank account, as expenses. In reality, they're investments in the future success of your business. When you have the right people around you, your opportunities to build long-term success expand exponentially. The money you spend in training and developing your team members will result in a stronger, more effective organization.

It takes much more than warm bodies to make a team. A team is a group of people who subscribe to a common mission. They are willing to work with and support each other for a greater good. This is the reason that your biggest task in team building is to effectively communicate your vision and values to the team.

We believe it is imperative to focus your team building efforts on those with shared vision, values and several other key traits. We also believe far too many entrepreneurs overemphasize the importance of skills and experience when hiring. People can learn new skills and can gain experience, but it is very difficult to "train" certain traits into someone...they either have it or they don't!

There are three traits that can't be taught, and that you shouldn't waste time trying to teach, that all of your potential team members must possess. These traits are motivation, integrity, and the capacity to grow.

Your team members must be motivated; they need to "bring it" each day and on every project. However, motivation without integrity is dangerous. You'll end up with someone who wants to get things done and achieve, but they are willing to cut corners and act against your core values to accomplish their goals. Finally, if you hire people who possess both motivation and integrity, but lack the capacity to grow, they will eventually slow down, or even stop, the forward progress of your organization.

One reason it's so important to hire people with these traits is that it only takes one bad team member to disrupt and poison an effective team. A person who lacks integrity will cost you customers and ultimately your reputation. An unmotivated team member is an anchor that will hold your organization down and adversely affect the morale of others.

Let's face it, no one enjoys firing team members, especially if that person is successful in some key areas, or possesses a skill that's difficult to acquire. Therefore, many business owners will turn a blind eye to the shortcomings of someone who's driving revenue. Our experience is that it's better to fire people quickly, before they have the chance to wreck the morale and effectiveness of the rest of the team. Our mantra is "slow to hire, quick to fire." That's not to say you should fire people for silly reasons, but when you see that someone isn't working out, be open and honest about it and let them go as humanely and as early as possible. Otherwise, you waste your valuable time and energy along with theirs. Don't let the right person for your team slip away because you're too busy trying to fix someone who is a bad fit.

> "...many business owners will turn a blind eye to the shortcomings of someone who's driving revenue."

Ensure that you protect yourself by having a written set of standard procedures in place that fully outlines your process for hiring, working with and, when needed, firing team members who aren't working out.

When you hire good people, allow them some freedom to maneuver. Give them the mission parameters: the goal, the timeline for completion, and any key touch points along the line. Empower them with the authority and autonomy necessary to succeed and then get out of the way! Let your team take over. Let them implement strategies to get everything done. Give them permission for a "touch and go" if they have questions or need clarification. Other than that, let them know you trust them to accomplish the goal.

Having a team like this frees you from the constant worry about things getting done, that slows down so many entrepreneurs. This is exciting, invigorating and freeing because it allows you to follow your passion and stay connected with why you became an entrepreneur in the first place!

CHAPTER 2

Strategy 5: Operations

Most businesses fail to create clear, easy to implement and repeatable systems within their businesses or, if developed, fail to employ them consistently. Not having proper systems in place from start-up forward prevents growth, lowers the value of the business to a potential future buyer and can ultimately lead to the utter failure of the business.

They may not be sexy or exciting to some, but certain operations are critical in order for your business to survive and thrive. First, let's define what we mean by operations. Operations are ongoing, repeatable activities that keep your business running smoothly. These activities include financial systems, sales lead generation and follow-through, inventory management, customer service, routine strategic planning, and anything else that your business repeats with any regularity throughout the year. In other words, operations encompasses just about everything you do to keep your business going!

Think of it this way: a soldier on the battlefield doesn't get to the front lines by himself and he has no chance of success if he tries to fight alone. In addition to the other soldiers around him, he has a team of supporting personnel: specialists who gather, interpret and disseminate intel, logisticians who work the supply lines from point of origin all the way to the foxhole, and communications experts who ensure maximum combat power is brought to bear with synchronicity. Without these systems functioning effectively in the background, the front line soldier doesn't have much hope for survival, not to mention success.

You may be thinking, "It's not life or death, why is this so important?

As long as I am growing sales and bringing in money, won't the back office stuff just take care of itself?"

We wish that were so! Unfortunately, we also know from painful personal experience that trying to operate any company, from a solo professional practice to a large multi-site organization with high complexity, is akin to wandering through a dense minefield with a blindfold on. Sooner or later, you are going to step on something very unpleasant with potentially disastrous results!

The good news? The benefits from taking the time and energy to create, implement and occasionally tweak systems are legion. Systemized operations result in greater profits, better customer service, more targeted marketing efforts, stronger team management and ultimately, a significantly more valuable company should you try to sell it as part of your exit strategy.

Let's look at a prime example that all successful entrepreneurs experience—the "Big Sale." A large sum of money from a major contract hits the top line, but actual profit turns out far lower than you anticipated. Where did the money go? For MVEs without effective cash flow systems, the usual answer is "I have no idea!"

When you have clear, repeatable systems in place for handling money as it comes in, you can track exactly where money goes in your company. For instance, you might find a hidden "money leech" in the form of unnecessary expenses, higher than expected travel costs or outsourcing over-rides that siphon away your profit. With the right system in place, you can quickly identify the leech and pour some strategic salt on it. Without good systems in place, the money leeches will eventually bleed you dry!

Solid systems are also a great way to reinforce gaps in your skill set or inherent strengths, freeing you to focus your energy to where you are strongest. Let's say you are great at getting the client to "yes" and closing the sales, if you can get in front of the client, but you aren't terribly strong in managing lead generation or sales call follow-up. Will you occasionally land a deal without a good system in place? Sure, but how much more effective will you be with a good lead generation system combined with a highly automated follow-up system?

Such a system, which can easily be run by a virtual team member with the right skill set, frees you to focus on your "core 20 percent" of highest and best time/energy use. Your team and supporting systems generate the leads, set-up the appointment, provide the pertinent pre-meeting intel and initiate the post-call, follow-up system based on the outcome of the initial meeting. You are now free of the constant struggle of front and back end sales cycle management and free to tackle more valuable strategic projects.

The long-term result? Greater revenue, more profits, a well-functioning team, and a happy MVE who isn't stuck in the weeds. You spend your time working ON the business, not IN the business.

Sounds pretty good, right? It is pretty good, but there is still that pesky short term challenge of putting time and effort into building these systems on the front-end. We won't lie to you; it's not easy for most MVEs to get past the initial inertia for putting these critical systems into place. The good news is others have already done much of the work for you (more on that later) and the benefits of having these systems in place far surpass the temporary inconvenience of creating them.

Fast forward in your mind to a time when your business is, indeed, operational and someone walks up to you on the street and offers you ten times revenue (a very generous offer) to purchase your business lock, stock and barrel on the condition it was a turnkey operation—all ready to go—will you be ready?

Effective systems provide you freedom, since you can step away for a week or even a month and be confident that the business will be able to run smoothly and produce revenue even while you're gone. The earlier you start systemizing, the easier it is to keep everything under control, so don't put it off!

So where do you begin? Each business is unique, so we can't give you absolute specifics on every system that your company needs. How-

ever, there are three critical areas for which you must commit to developing good operations. The first area is cash flow. We cannot stress enough the importance of understanding your cash flow. At the most basic level, you need to know how much money comes in and where it goes. Unfortunately, many entrepreneurs don't have a firm handle on their cash flow. They may have a ballpark idea of how much is coming in the front door, but possess no clarity around where it goes afterwards and don't have a clue whether it's being spent effectively or not.

Cash flow systems allow you to keep accurate records, which is always very important at tax time. Obviously, you want to avoid trouble with local, state and federal tax agencies for failing to properly handle income or payroll taxes. At the same time, you want to ensure that you are taking advantage of all legitimate deductions.

The second area is what we term "professional operations." Many MVEs unwittingly expose themselves to unnecessary legal liability. You might be using decade-old contracts with outdated language or be out of compliance with required local, state or federal regulatory requirements for your industry.

REGULARLY CHECK-IN WITH A LEGAL ADVISOR

Regular check-ups with a legal advisor can easily confirm whether or not you are in compliance with any new laws, using up-to-date documents and availing yourself of the best business entity to ensure adequate legal protections. Without the correct system in place, the check-ups won't happen and these items could easily fall through the cracks.

The third area is personnel. **Key areas to consider around your personnel system** include:

1 Hiring

2 Prerequisite candidate qualifications

3 Explanation of introductory period

4 Performance review

5 Benefits/compensation packages

Your personnel systems should also help you determine whether a certain position is bringing value to your organization? Many companies have no system in place to measure these key areas.

It's daunting to think about building all these systems from scratch. Fortunately, if you invest some exploratory intel time, you'll discover many of the systems you need already exist and are successfully supporting businesses just like yours.

Examples include:

SYSTEMS IN PLACE SO YOU DON'T HAVE TO REINVENT THE WHEEL

1 Computer systems
2 Specialized software programs
3 Human resources manuals
4 Consulting agreement templates
5 Virtual call centers to answer your calls with a live, human voice
6 Client Relationship Management (CRM) software
7 Sales lead generation software
8 Marketing software

You'll find that 90-95% of the systems that you need to start or grow your business are available "off the shelf" and require little or no customization. You and/or your team will need to put some time in tweaking the last few pieces specific to your business. Be warned, however: don't automatically default to the lowest cost version available for each system.

While understandable, since it costs money to purchase software or hire a systems consultant, this poverty mindset can really hurt you in the long run. **Before finalizing your purchase decision, ask yourself these questions:**

How much money will I waste **not** having the right systems in place?

How much time will I throw away doing the same things over and over again?

How much will I lose if I open myself up to a lawsuit because my contracts aren't up to date?

Remember, developing, purchasing, and implementing the right systems is an investment in your business, not an expense. In addition, enormous strides are taking place almost daily in scalable, highly customizable technology solutions that allow you to run most businesses from anywhere in the world with a smartphone, a laptop and a reliable internet connection.

Good systems create great opportunities: a primary reason most MVEs go into business is to create a good life for their families. Earlier in the section, we shared how systems will make you more profitable, enabling you to track your cash flow and eliminate the money leeches draining your profits. We also shared how automating systems will save you substantial time in the long run. What's the end result? Systems actually allow you to enjoy that better life with your family instead of spending it at the office!

Understanding the value of systems is just as important if you plan to purchase an existing company. Ensure that you fully investigate the organization's systems from top to bottom. If you find out there's nothing under the hood, either walk away or negotiate a deeply discounted price. Also, make sure the purchase agreement you sign stipulates that you are buying all the systems that come with that company. If needed, negotiate that the previous owner (or other key personnel) stays on board for a set period of time, to train you in the essential systems for the business. The previous owner can stay for a week, a month, or whatever period of time you believe necessary. The main thing is that you understand the systems of that business so you can hit the ground running!

Key Operation Concepts

✓ Effective, repeatable and easy-to-implement systems are key to long-term success

✓ Great systems substantially increase the value of companies being built to sell

✓ Scalability and leverage require effective systems

✓ Coaches help you drastically reduce your learning curve.

Strategy 6: Rapid Action

We've all heard the expression, "knowledge is power." It's an old saying and many people believe it. Unfortunately, there's one small problem; it's a lie. Don't believe it for a second. The truth is that action is power. You can hook your brain up to the Library of Congress and download every bit of information residing there, and it won't do you a bit of good until you act on that knowledge. Success comes to doers, not dreamers!

Action delivers results. Action creates opportunities. Action dampens potential fall-out from the occasional (but inevitable) error. Taking rapid, decisive action is the single greatest differentiator between barely surviving and truly thriving.

We can't over stress the importance of taking rapid action. We see too many aspiring MVEs who are in a holding pattern, waiting for just the right opportunity, waiting for just a little more information, waiting to finish the formal business plan or adding the last touches to the website, waiting for the perfect alignment of the stars. Something prevents them from shifting out of neutral, taking action and moving forward. We know top achievers in many different industries. Men and women who create positive change, run great organizations, experience explosive growth, and are continually innovating. They share few common exterior traits: They have different heights, weights, ethnicities, political leanings and education levels. The single salient strength that ties top achievers together is getting things done. Fast!

The ability to take rapid, decisive action is more important than intelligence, education and raw talent. In many ways, it is the single best predictor of the level of success that you will achieve, both in business and in life. We often find MVEs sitting at the starting line idling because they are waiting on some external factor, such as the government approving a big contract, the bank finalizing a financing package or a team member finishing a proposal. They fixate completely on clearing this one perceived hurdle to moving their business forward and everything grinds to a halt.

We celebrate dreamers in our culture. The self-help shelves at bookstores are packed with titles directing us to follow our dreams. Dreamers create transformative ideas that lead to great advancements in every area of business and life. That said, dreaming alone isn't enough and any cursory study of leading change agents reveals they take decisive action to turn dreams into reality.

MVEs must be doers, as well as dreamers. This transition is difficult when coming from a W-2 paycheck environment, where you receive a regular paycheck even if you aren't working all that hard to earn it. As an entrepreneur you don't have the luxury to slack off; your income relates directly to the amount of positive activity in which you engage. If you get lazy as an entrepreneur, you end up with no food on the table!

Wouldn't it be great if you had a clearly defined target and perfect sight picture in mind each time before you took action? Unfortunately, today's dynamic business battlefield offers few perfect looks or sure things. We've already shared how waiting for perfect alignment is a direct route to the poor house, so you must develop some comfort level with moving out and taking course corrective action as you go forward.

Of course, by employing these strategies you aren't taking action blindly. By following the strategies already discussed, you've applied some brainpower to:

■ Developing the vision for your organization.

■ Researching and analyzing appropriate intel.

■ Connecting with coaches, mentors and advisors.

■ Building the right team.

■ Getting the right systems in place.

> "Perfectionism is the mortal enemy of the entrepreneur..."

Is there a perfect time to take action? Absolutely not! There's no such thing as the perfect time to do anything. Perfectionism is the mortal enemy of the entrepreneur and those that attempt to attain it end up mighty frustrated. Even if you manage to craft the perfect plan and arrange perfect circumstances, they only remain perfect while on paper. It starts breaking down the moment you implement and make contact with external forces. Check the quote at the top of this section, "No battle plan survives contact with the enemy intact.

This is just as true in business as in combat. You'll need to improvise, adapt and take course-corrective action. You might need a small course adjustment of five to 10 degrees, or a complete U-turn. Figure it out in stride and keep moving. If you stop every 10 feet to reanalyze everything, others will fly past you in terms of success.

The competition may not be as smart as or well-educated as you. They may not have your network, or financial backing or support systems. Their product or service might not be anywhere near as good as yours. But if they have developed the habit of rapid action and are continuously moving forward, they will consistently beat you to market and co-opt your clients/ customers. All because they initiated their imperfect plan and took decisive action!

So what should you do? Our advice is to simply get moving! Connect with your vision, goals and intel to determine the initial direction and get rolling. Focus your marketing on those you believe are most interested in your product or service (just remember, target what they want, not what you think they need). Look for low hanging fruit and take on targets of opportunity as you go. People are often surprised at how easily clients/customers appear once they get into action.

As you're rolling, take note of what's working and what isn't. Refine your message or shift your market to zero in on your most receptive audience, and discard pre-conceived notions that don't pan out. This "build the airplane as you fly" approach is incredibly uncomfortable for some MVEs, but is critically important, especially if you are in start-up or rapid growth mode.

This approach is the business equivalent of recon by fire. In combat, when a unit believes a certain area is a likely enemy position, the unit may open fire on that position, hoping to provoke a reaction from the enemy. As an entrepreneur, sometimes you must do exactly the same thing. If you believe you can successfully compete in a market segment, you need to engage and open fire on that segment (figuratively speaking, of course).

Engaging the market can take many forms, depending on your resources, skill set, support team and the market itself. Focused (and low-cost) marketing, speaking appearances, and joint ventures with a complimentary business already enjoying success in the market are all solid strategies. If you are correct and it's a target-rich environment, your message will start resonating and gaining traction, allowing you to expand your business.

Remember, fortune favors those who take action. We know scores of MVEs who started moving down the entrepreneurial road with one concept and discovered a far more lucrative opportunity right around the first bend.

Action creates and attracts opportunity: Unfortunately, we also know a fair number who just sit on

> "No amount of positive thinking or self-affirmation will cause opportunities to fall from the sky and drop into your lap. **Action creates and attracts opportunities.**"

the road, convinced of the brilliance of their own ideas and waiting for business to come to them. No amount of positive thinking or self-affirmation will cause opportunities to fall from the sky and drop into your lap (no matter what the Law of Attraction says). Action creates and attracts opportunities.

Use these **three simple exercises** any time you feel yourself getting stuck or frustrated:

ACTION EXERCISE #1: Go for Progress, Not Perfection

Understand, accept, and internalize the fact that there is no perfect plan. Even your most meticulous plans won't survive contact on the business battlefield, so stop trying to be perfect! Get moving in the direction of making your vision a reality and keep your head up, looking for opportunities. Today's business is so dynamic that the only constant is change. Technology, market and economic conditions, new applications for existing products/services, and the wants of clients and customers are always in motion. To succeed, you must be moving, too!

ACTION EXERCISE #2: Don't Try to Eat the Elephant in One Bite:

We often fail to take action because the task before us seems too daunting, like trying to eat an entire elephant in one sitting. The solution? Try breaking seemingly overwhelming tasks into smaller chunks and dig into the bite-sized pieces with gusto! Once you start knocking out the smaller pieces, you'll find the big task looks much less menacing. Also, don't be afraid to start with something small. Sometimes, just doing something relatively simple, like making a phone call to schedule an appointment with a potential client, gives you the motivation you need to attack the larger project. Action fuels motivation!

ACTION EXERCISE #3: The More You Act, the Easier It Gets:

Developing your "action habit muscle" is just like any other exercise in building strength or cardiovascular endurance. The more you take action, the stronger you become and the easier it becomes. This is the primary reason that breaking overwhelming tasks into bite-sized pieces works so well. You accomplish one small task, and then another and then another. Before long, you'll notice you are thinking differently and actively looking for new reasons and ways to act, instead of making excuses for why you can't.

Key Rapid Action Concepts

✔ Analysis paralysis will doom your business.

✔ It's far better to take action and course correct than stand idle.

✔ There is no such thing as a perfect plan.

Strategy 7: You

The first six strategies (Vision, Intel, Coaching, Team, Ops and Rapid Action) are essential elements of building long-term success in business, but unless you apply the ideas in this section, the other strategies won't matter. When you strip everything else away, your success—in your business and in your life—depends on **you**!

> "Why do you want to live the entrepreneurial life style?"

Think of the other principles as spokes in a wheel. You are the hub of that wheel. No matter how strong the spokes are, the wheel will eventually fall apart if the hub isn't sound. In this section we'll share what it takes to build a business, and a life, of long-lasting significance.

Why do you want to live the entrepreneurial lifestyle? At the most basic level, of course, the majority of us desire to create a stream of income that supports the kind of life we want for our family and ourselves. Most of us want to support charities and causes that we believe in.

Finally, many of us want to use our experience and talents to leave the world better than how we found it. When you look at the sacrifice and dedication it takes to successfully start and grow a small business, you know there is more involved than just making a living. After all, you are signing up for a roller-coaster ride of ups and downs, victories and defeats, frustration and euphoria and most of these come before 0900 each morning!

This also ties into the vision you have for your organization, as well as your personal vision for your life. Remember, vision is not something that you think about once and then hide away in your desk drawer. Keep the reasons you do what you do front and center and refer to them often, especially when things get tough.

To achieve long-term success, you must understand the priorities that virtually all high achievers make routine habits. Connect with these priorities and try to make them so second-nature that they are always operating in the background of everything you do. The following **three priorities can literally make you unstoppable**, if you choose to embrace them. **They are:**

SELF-DISCIPLINE: Self-discipline, in this context, means that you pursue excellence in everything you or your company does. The entrepreneurial lifestyle won't work for you if mediocre is good enough in your book. Committing to excellence builds customer loyalty, attracts world-class team members and differentiates you in the marketplace. At its core, self-discipline means making decisions based on what's right; not what feels good at the moment. The right decisions benefit your clients/customers, your team and honor your vision and values instead of surrendering to expediency and convenience. Self-disciplined leaders make conscious, deliberate decisions and avoid cutting corners or compromising principles to squeeze a few extra dollars from a transaction.

TENACITY: Tenacity is simply not giving up, no matter the circumstance. Tenacity is refusing to allow opposition, uncertainty, and the occasional failure stop you. Any time you move forward and upset the status quo, you will likely face adversity. The question is: what will you do about it?

When you encounter opposition, failure or adversity, you have two options. You can quit, which is always the wrong option; or you can regroup, learn from your mistakes, and move forward. Unfortunately, many entrepreneurs throw in the towel the very first time they run into a real challenge. We strongly believe tenacity sets most MVEs apart from other entrepreneurs, since we understand that adversity and temporary failure makes us stronger. Never give up and never surrender!

COMMITMENT TO SELF-DEVELOPMENT: The skills and knowledge required to successfully navigate business start-ups are not the same skills you will need to take the business to the next level. In truth, if you are not continuously growing as a leader, you will eventually stifle your company's success. Don't be the anchor or lodestone that weighs the company down: set the example through continuous learning and growth.

How do you keep growing as a leader? You have many options. Commit to reading a certain number of leadership/business books per year. Go to leadership seminars and boot camps. Pursue a professional designation that is noteworthy in your industry. In reality, exactly how you do it is less important than your commitment to doing it!

••

One final priority we strongly suggest you establish in your business from day one is uncompromising ethics. We encourage you to set and maintain the highest possible ethical standards for both yourself and your company.

Not long ago, Time magazine declared the first decade of the 21st century as the "Decade from Hell." How did they come to this conclusion? One key factor was the extensive financial upheaval and corruption prevalent during the decade. Think Enron, WorldCom, the dot-com boom and bust, Lehmann Brothers, Bernie Madoff, and a whole host of similar sordid characters. There are literally dozens of examples during this time period of people taking ethical shortcuts to obtain short-term success, often ruining hundreds or thousands of lives in the process.

Of course, the media and popular culture feeds right into the perception that all business owners are crooks out for a quick profit at another's expense. In movies, business leaders are typically portrayed as one-dimensional villains, looking to make money by any means available, legal or illegal.

In reality, business people who fit that description are quite rare. Most business owners care deeply about their customers. They care about their employees. They are very involved in their communities and their families. Unfortunately, those villain stereotypes still persist. A tiny fraction of unscrupulous business leaders allow their low ethical standards to taint the reputation of the vast majority of honest, hardworking business leaders.

Many, if not most, of these disgraced business leaders started off as basically honest people. At some point though, they chose to cut corners. Maybe they told a little white lie to a client to close a deal. Perhaps they took credit for something they didn't do, to get a promotion they didn't deserve. Ethical lapses usually start small and then grow until they take over the life of the person committing them.

The best way to keep from going down that road is to set your moral and ethical standards at the very beginning of your career. You must decide from the start that you won't cut corners, no matter what.

This is where your ethical standards tie into the self-discipline we mentioned in the last section. You cannot make decisions based on how you feel in the moment or what's expedient. In the heat of the battle, you might feel like throwing ethics out the window in order to make a quick sale, especially if your business is having a really tight month.

You must decide beforehand that you will always occupy the highest moral ground. Stress the values important to your company, even during the interview process. The best time to weed out people who don't share your ethical standards is before you hire them. If you find that one of your team members cuts ethical corners, even in minor areas, don't ignore it, look the other way and hope things will straighten themselves out. They won't! Deal with the situation swiftly and decisively.

It's difficult to discipline or even terminate an employee, especially one who makes money for the company. Minor ethical lapses are dangerous for a number of reasons. One reason is that a team member who will lie to, or cheat a customer in order to gain an advantage will do the same to you. You may profit from this employee's misdeeds at first, but cleaning up their mess will cost you far more in the long run.

To achieve enduring success, you must build on the foundation of the highest ethical standards. People, customers and team members alike, want to attach themselves to a company that's clear about what it stands for, and does what it says it will do. Unfortunately, there aren't many companies that strive to maintain those standards, so you'll stand out in your industry!

How many people will you actually touch in your lifetime? Far more than you probably think. Your "Sphere of Influence" includes everyone you touch as you go through life. You have the ability to affect the lives of everyone in your Sphere of Influence, either positively or negatively. Of course, that includes your family and friends. It also includes your vendors, your employees, your customers and your neighbors.

If you operate your business and your life by pursuing excellence and the highest ethical standards, your Sphere of Influence is going to be positively affected. But if you start cheating people and your business goes under, many people will be negatively affected. You should find that extremely motivating. You can positively affect hundreds, if not thousands, of people simply by sticking to your vision and values.

One of the best ways we know for a person to start thinking about their legacy is to consider their own funeral. It may sound a little morbid, but think about these questions: What do you want people to say about you after you die? What do you want your family to say? What about your team members, or your business competitors? Which charities will show their appreciation because of your contributions?

It's sobering to think in these terms, but we believe it's the best way to get you to concentrate on the kind of life you want to live. Once you visualize what you want to happen, it's time to take the next step. Decide what you need to do in order to build the legacy you visualized when you thought of your own funeral. Begin building that life today, so that when the end of your life comes, your legacy will be assured.

Key You Concepts

✓ Focusing on and operating from your inherent strengths is fundamental to long-term success.

✓ Strong ethics makes for good business.

✓ Your sphere of influence—positive or negative—is far larger than you think.

Veteran Business Owner Profile

NAME: Liz Perez

PROGRAM: Entrepreneurship Bootcamp for Veterans with Disabilities (EBV),Texas A&M University, Class of 2011

BRANCH: U.S. Navy

BUSINESS: GC Green

Liz Perez is a U.S. Navy Petty Officer who was influenced by the military as a young child on a U.S. Army base during the Cold and Gulf Wars. Her father, who served for almost 20 years in the Army, was medically discharged shortly after serving in Desert Storm. He passed away soon after and was his daughter's inspiration to join the Navy.

In the Navy, Liz was an aviation logistics specialist. During a deployment, she received injuries from a 25-foot fall while inspecting cargo coming off of a ship. After several deployments, and being struck with the realities of war as a child, the adult Liz saw life through a different lens.

"Losing my father was tough, but when I lost a friend on the USS Cole, this is when things became 'real' for me. It has inspired me to do something in my life in their honor, and this is why I started GC Green," she says.

GC Green (Green Build General Contracting and Consulting Firm), is a successful consulting firm that Liz owns. Her business is involved in an effort to broaden the outreach and impact of the green economy. The focus of the firm is to be part of the solution to become less energy dependent as a nation, by training and educating veterans in the clean energy jobs sector.

The business provides apprenticeships and project placement opportunities in energy efficiency and alternative energy systems for veterans and displaced workers throughout California. GC Green recently won a statewide contract to provide BPI BA training under Energy Upgrade California. In addition, the firm conducts home energy retrofits in Southern California that include a workforce of veterans.

Learn more about GC Green at *gcgreen.com.*

CHAPTER 3

Finding and Acting on the "Right" Opportunity

> "The fundamental reason that any new company exists is to take advantage of an opportunity."

T his chapter provides insight into the skills and activities related to recognizing whether or not your idea or business concept is one that can be leveraged to create a viable and sustainable business venture.

Differences Between an Opportunity and an "Idea"

The fundamental reason that any new company exists is to take advantage of an opportunity. As an aspiring entrepreneur, it is necessary to understand how to think about real opportunities, where these opportunities come from, and how to spot opportunities.

FUNDAMENTALS OF VALUE CREATION: OPPORTUNITY & IDEA

Simply speaking, an opportunity is a problem plus a solution (opportunity = problem + solution). The problem is a customer problem, something that is real and knowable, and the solution is something that solves that problem and creates value for customers.

The formal definition of opportunity states that opportunity has the qualities of being attractive, durable, and timely and is anchored in a product or service that creates or adds value for its buyers or end users. To elaborate on these attributes: attractive means something that would be of interest to the customers; durable means that there needs to be a value to customers that has some staying power; timely means that it has to happen now or soon—not 10 years from now; anchored means that it is something that can be done via product or service, i.e. the solution. Finally, create value shows that there is a need for the problem.

> **Opportunity** has the qualities of being attractive, durable, and timely and is anchored in a product or service that creates or adds value for its buyers or end users.

Examples of Opportunity:

The problem that **Puffs** identified was that when people have colds and wipe their noses with facial tissues, their noses become red and irritated. Puffs' solution was to put lotion in their facial tissues and solve the problem.

Tostitos recognized that more and more people are health conscious and even though chips are delicious, they are not healthy. The solution that Tostitos came up with was baked chips, which are healthier than fried chips. Another problem that Tostitos identified was that salsa or dip falls off of flat chips, so their additional solution was to make their chips scooped. The scoops work like a bowl and prevent spillage. They solved two customer problems using one product with two solutions: Baked Tostitos Scoops.

A common problem among athletes and physically active people is the loss of electrolytes, water, and other nutrients when they train, workout, or are being very active. **Gatorade** created a solution to this problem by developing a water product with electrolytes, sugar, and other nutrients that is easy to absorb and replenishes the body.

WINDOW OF OPPORTUNITY FOR MARKET ENTRY

For an entrepreneur to capitalize on an opportunity, the window of opportunity has to be open. The term "window of opportunity" is a metaphor which describes a period of time during which an opportunity must be acted on or missed, a time in which a firm can realistically enter a new market. Once the market for a new opportunity, be it a product or service, is established, its window of opportunity opens. As the market grows, firms compete to enter the market to establish a profitable position. At some point, the market matures. The opportunity is then exploited and not durable anymore, and this is when the window of opportunity closes. The notion of a window that opens for a while and then closes highlights the fleeting nature of opportunities, where timing and the attractiveness of the product and/or service is essential. Too early might be as bad as too late.

There are numerous windows of opportunity that entrepreneurs need to consider. These include market, legislature, competition, and technology, among others. Some might be more important than others, and entrepreneurs need to get the timing right to get through the window(s) that matter.

Many entrepreneurs assume that timing is everything and they want to be first in identifying and exploiting the opportunity, but many times there are other factors, as mentioned previously, such as competition, customers, and external sources (technology, legislature, policies, etc.). An example of a window of opportunity and timing is the Internet search engine industry. Yahoo was one of the first Internet search engine websites that started exploiting the opportunity in the mid-1990s, together with Northernstar, Alta Vista, and others. Even though they were the first in the market, a new player, Google, joined the industry with new technology in 1998, conquered the market opportunity, and still owns the market today. At present, the opportunity is closed, the market has matured, and even Microsoft's attempts to introduce Bing were not very successful, since Google has been leveraging their technology and brand recognition to keep the window of opportunity closed.

Entrepreneurs need to understand that there is a difference between an opportunity and an idea. An idea is a thought, light bulb moment, feeling, or notion. However, not every idea will meet the criteria of an opportunity. It is essential to dig deeper and study the feasibility of the idea. Many entrepreneurs have failed; not because they didn't work hard, but very often they failed because there was no real opportunity for the venture that they started.

CHAPTER 3

WHY WOULD SOMETHING NOT BE A GOOD OPPORTUNITY?

There are many ways that entrepreneurs can reflect upon their ideas and test if they are good opportunities, or not. Entrepreneurs should be aware of the following reasons that explain why an idea will not be a good opportunity:

■ **NO MARKET NEED** Do we really need a better mouse trap? Is it worth investing the time and effort in coming up with a better mouse trap, if the existing one has been effective, simple, and one can buy them in a pack of four for 99 cents?

Window of Opportunity is a period of time during which an opportunity must be acted on or missed.

■ **CUSTOMERS NOT DISSATISFIED** A customer is the most important person in any business; if you have no customers, then you are not in business. If the competition has products and services that are meeting the demands of the customers, and the customers are satisfied, they will not switch to your products and/or services.

■ **STRONG CUSTOMER LOYALTY** Loyal customers return to products and/or services despite other offers from the competition. It might cost a new company a lot of time and effort to impress the customer, and they still may not get enough customers to switch and make it a profitable business.

■ **CUSTOMER "SWITCHING COSTS"** These are costs incurred when a customer changes from one supplier or marketplace to another. The higher these costs are, the more difficult it is to execute the switch. If a business sells something that customers can't get elsewhere—at least not easily—then that business has high customer switching costs. For example, if you have only one grocery store in your neighborhood, and you don't own a car, then you'd be willing to pay extra to buy your food there. To get to another store, you'd have to walk a long way. Thus, there are high "costs" to switching to a different grocery store. In this scenario, the grocery store can charge higher prices and generate excess profits. Another example is cell phone contracts: if you sign the two-year contract that customers typically sign to get a deal on a phone and later you want to break the contract, you have to pay a high cancellation fee. The cancellation fee is higher than the perceived deal that you would get with other cell phone companies, hence the switching cost is high and the customer sticks with the original cell phone company. Accordingly, be aware of your competition, what customers are purchasing, and know if the switching costs will prohibit them from switching to your products and/or services.

■ **CUSTOMERS HARD TO REACH** If your customers are not accessible and the effort to deliver your product or service to them is costly, so much that it will not allow you to make a profit, then it may not be feasible to pursue that customer. For example, if you want to offer energy/electricity in rural areas, where folks use generators, you might have to spend a lot of money to develop an infrastructure. The number of customers is low compared to the distances between the houses and facilities that would need energy, so the cost of the infrastructure and its maintenance becomes high compared to the revenues.

■ **INTENSE COMPETITION** Direct competition is when products or services performing the same function compete against each other. For example, one brand of pick-up trucks competes with several other brands of pick-up trucks. Sometimes, two companies are rivals and one adds new products to their line, which leads to another company distributing the same new things, and in this manner they compete. However, if you have a high number of competitors that have strong brand recognition, it will be very difficult to enter the market with a new brand and manufacturer. In the case of pick-up trucks, the competition among Ford, Chevy, GM, Toyota, and Dodge is already intense because they offer competitive prices, financing, warranties, customer services, and much more, so it would be very difficult for a new competitor to enter the market.

■ **EASY FOR PEOPLE TO ENTER AFTER YOU** A business whose products or services are easily replicable has a high chance of competitors coming after the same opportunity because it is easily done and does not cost much to be done. A new settlement that will need grass cutting services is an example. Even if you are first today, tomorrow you will be competing with kids from the neighborhood, landscaping companies, handyman services, and many others, who will start advertising and potentially beating you in price.

■ **CUSTOMERS TOO DEMANDING RELATIVE TO WHAT THEY'LL PAY** If the business is catering to very demanding customers, oftentimes the time and effort invested in those customers shows no return, and the company loses not only in profits, but also risks losing reputation and credibility.

■ **WINDOW NOT OPEN** One needs to be aware of whether the window of opportunity has closed, the opportunity has passed (i.e. Internet search engines), or the window of opportunity is currently closed, though it will open in five years, for example 'space tourism'. If it has passed, then all investments will be lost, since there is no opportunity to make a profit. Furthermore, if one starts a company and the window of opportunity has not opened, it might have a further effect on the company besides loss of revenues and investments. To name a few: supplier relations might be damaged, the company's credibility might be questioned in the future, and the team dynamic might change, causing some smart people to leave the team.

Entrepreneurship as a Problem-Solution Relationship

Opportunities don't have to be magical, technologically-advanced issues. One only needs to look around to encounter numerous opportunities. We are all surrounded by dozens of opportunities; however, we either do not see them or do not act on them. Usually, the best opportunities are based on problems that irritate, challenge, and bore people on a regular basis, yet they don't do anything to solve these issues. This chapter will focus on these problems, where they can be found, and how one can identify and analyze them, understanding the factors and elements that create entrepreneurial opportunities from these problems.

PROBLEMS AS A SOURCE OF OPPORTUNITY

Problems or challenges that people face every day are great sources of opportunities. As an entrepreneur, ask yourself: What are your biggest "bugs"? These can be simple things, such as long lines at the gym, access to healthy food at work, your video game is fun only for one week, and the list continues. What implication might the long line at the gym have for you as an entrepreneur? There is definitely a high demand, so is there an opportunity for another gym? Or, might there be an opportunity to develop an application for gym users to reserve equipment before they go to the gym? Or, an application for gyms to measure the needs based on the customers' demographics and usage data? Further, the lack of healthy food at work: what opportunities can this provide for an entrepreneur? Maybe to open a healthy deli that can deliver healthy food to the business district? Or, to create healthy frozen dishes that can be microwaved during lunch hours in the offices and distribute them through local grocery stores?

FINDING OPPORTUNITY

1 Challenge existing problems

2 Look for patterns of trends (in markets, demographics, social behaviors, customer buying behavior, competitive practices, etc.)

3 Monitor changes in rules, laws, regulations

4 Conduct 'needs' research, focus on problems

5 Look for under-utilized resources

Example: College Bed Lofts

College Bed Lofts was started due to a lack of space in campus dorm rooms for students. Today, College Bed Lofts sells about 5,000 lofts a year as a simple solution to a space problem.

Think about 'technical' challenges that you might face; for example, sweat/moisture weighs down your gym clothes, running out of memory on your DVR, your computer freezes when streaming video, and so on. How can these be translated into potential opportunities? Considering the example of the sweat/moisture weighing down your gym clothes when you play basketball or work out; what are potential solutions to this problem? One of the solutions would be to develop a clothing material, which will not allow the moisture to collect and weigh down your clothing.

Example: One True Media

One True Media was started by Mark Moore due to his frustration in managing the explosion of photos generated by digital cameras. Hard disks and tiny digital cameras and camera phones lacked the storage ability to realistically manage the photos. Alternatives such as hard disks were inadequate as well. One True Media allowed users to store their photos online, package, print, and share with others.

CHAPTER 3

Think about "big picture" things, such as high energy costs, waste that comes with all packaging, paperwork at every office, and so on. Considering the problem of energy costs, as an entrepreneur you want to ask yourself how these costs can be reduced. One way could be solar panels or wind turbines that can be mounted on the house, which in the long run will reduce the costs of energy, while having a positive impact on the environment overall. Another opportunity would be to provide services which will test houses for energy loss and consult homeowners in terms of what they need to do in order to make their homes more energy efficient.

. . . .

Example: Overstock.com

O verstock.com The founders of Overstock.com recognized a problem that many e-tailers had, namely too much inventory, and that they needed a place or channel to dump the excess inventory Instead of selling it off at cheaper prices to end consumers—potentially hurting their own brand recognition-they can sell it to Overstock.com.

. . . .

Making a list of these problems/challenges will help entrepreneurs to start to thinking about problems that might be worth solving.

TRENDS AS OPPORTUNITY CREATORS

Trends are another source of opportunity. As an entrepreneur, it is important that you look at what is going on around you and how things are changing. Change is oftentimes the source of new needs and problems. These changes can generally be classified into one of four different areas of trends: social factors, economic factors, technological advances, and political/ regulatory changes.

■ SOCIAL TRENDS

The social factors that contain opportunities include the customs, lifestyles, culture, and values that characterize a society. Social factors also include anything within the context of society that has the potential for new opportunity, such as changes in population demographics, rising educational levels, shifts in norms and values, and attitudes toward social responsibility.

Changes in population demographics have many potential consequences in terms of need for new products or services, living standards, living needs, and other behavior, which are all sources for new market opportunities. As the total population changes, the demand for products and services also changes. For example, the decline in the birthrate and improvement in health care have contributed to an increase in the average age of the population in the U.S. Increase of the senior citizen, i.e. Baby Boomer population, increases demand for certain products. For example, they prefer to live in ranches rather than two-story homes, due to stairs and easy access, and they do not need a big house since they are empty nesters (they live alone, kids have moved out); hence, the opportunity is to build two- or three-bedroom ranch homes that are accessible. Most senior citizens are retired and looking for ways that they can spend their time; therefore, there is also an entertainment opportunity such as travel tours, for senior citizens.

Another example of population change is the increase in different immigrant groups in the U.S. that have different needs and face problems of buying products or receiving services that they are accustomed to, or that they can understand and relate to. For example, an increase in the Spanish-speaking population might provide opportunities to offer small business consulting services in Spanish, or advertising opportunities for small businesses, i.e. brochures, websites, and newspaper ads in Spanish in order to reach that population.

Rising educational levels is another social factor that provides new opportunities. Higher educational levels allow people to earn higher incomes than would have been possible otherwise. The increase in income creates opportunities to purchase additional goods and services, and to raise the overall standard of living of a large segment of the population. Increase in income provides people with more disposable income, which they can use on vacation homes, additional cars (i.e. sports cars or convertibles), investments, luxury clothing, jewelry, and the list goes on. The key is identifying the problems or gaps in product/ service offerings that these people face and coming up with a solution, an opportunity.

Another social factor is social responsibility, which is the expectation that a business or individual will strive to improve the welfare of society and its environment. With growing awareness and the urge to become more environmentally friendly and sustain the resources that we have on earth, there are growing needs, problems, and gaps that are creating many business opportunities for new and existing companies.

More companies are adding new, environmentally friendly products or are switching completely to become green. One can see a change in products offered at most local grocery stores, as the shelves are packed with 'all natural' or 'organic' products. Parents, if they can, are choosing organic products for their children, to provide them with healthy nutrition. Over the last decade there have been numerous new and existing small companies that have leveraged this trend and created new products and services. For example, The Better Food Company introduced healthy snacks where all ingredients are organic and all natural. Tostitos, on the other hand, has introduced baked chips, which are healthier than fried chips, to address the needs of health conscious customers.

Furthermore, car companies are developing and manufacturing green cars, i.e. hybrids, which are gaining in popularity due to their low emissions, as well as their savings on climbing gas costs. At the same time, these companies have started to use recycled materials when manufacturing a new car, which creates a perceived social responsibility of the company amongst potential buyers.

ECONOMIC FORCES

Previously, it was identified that rising educational levels open new opportunities for people to earn higher income, and that higher income causes an increase in the level of disposable income. An increase in disposable income is an economic force that creates opportunities. When incomes are high, people are more willing to buy products and services that enhance their lives. With disposable income, people tend to travel more, purchase items (such as hot tubs, swimming pools, home entertainment systems, or a second car), and many other products that are considered luxury items, and otherwise would not be purchased.

Different economic sectors have direct impacts on how people spend their money. For example, when the value of the U.S. dollar falls, one can expect an increase of foreign tourism in the U.S. and at the same time, we can see an increase in export of U.S. goods. Another example is the interest rate. When interest rates fall, one can expect to see an increase in housing sales and at the same time, an increase in construction developments. When the interest rate increases, one will see a decline in housing sales and an increase in housing rental demand, which in turn might cause an increase in rental cost due to increased demand.

Identifying economic forces and the opportunities caused by them requires a better understanding of the people who are affected by these causes. For example, an increase in the disposable income amongst women provided an opportunity for Lowe's to target women, who are decision makers when it comes to numerous Do-It-Yourself (DIY) projects within the household, such as kitchen remodeling, bathroom remodeling, painting, and so on. Similarly, as more seniors are  retiring, the demand increases for the products and services they buy and use. For example, one can expect to see an increase in new golf courses and an increase in sales of golf equipment and accessories.

ADVANCES IN TECHNOLOGY

Technological advances can provide opportunities to help satisfy basic needs in a better, more convenient way. Once new technology is created, new products to advance it are usually not far behind. For example, the first smart phone provided opportunities for new applications to make the use of the phone more effective, while at the same time allowing users to solve some problems and needs. One example of this is "Grocery Smart," a shopping list application that gets rid of the physical notes and paper clips, allowing the user to speak while the application automatically updates the list in the phone. It can be used by numerous users, simultaneously allowing all family members to add groceries to the list; hence, it saves time, requires fewer efforts, addresses everyone's grocery needs, and decreases the stress in finding paper and pencil and remembering where the list actually is; simple problem, simple solution, more than 200,000 users.

POLITICAL/REGULATORY CHANGES

Political action and regulatory changes also provide opportunities for entrepreneurs. New laws, political instability, and global terrorism have all provided business opportunities. A good example of this would be the need for more and advanced security for companies and governments looking to protect physical assets and intellectual property from attack.

Another example of political action and regulatory change is the company Vlingo, which created  hands free texting for cell phones due to laws prohibiting texting while driving. This example also shows how advances in technology have made texting popular and have provided an opportunity for this company to solve the problem of texting while driving by using a voice recognition technology.

AREA	THINGS TO LOOK FOR	EXAMPLES
Economic Forces	• Spending patterns • Disposable income • Economic climate	• Gasbuddy.com to find cheap gas • Jetblue for low cost flights • Designer clothes for teens with more cash
Social Trends	• Demographics • Education • Fads and priorities for people	• Services for Baby Boomers • Social networking • Green products • Healthy organic food
Technological Advances	• Emerging technologies • New uses of established technology	• Cell phone/PDA advances • Alternative energies • Nanotechnology • 3D movies and games
Political and Regulatory Changes	• New laws • Foreign trade rules • Changes in government	• Products that exceed safety standards • Electronic health records • Software vendors to deal with Sarbanes-Oxley Act

FILL THE GAPS

Many large firms are looking for big problems and broad markets, since big problems provide big opportunities. For example, companies such as Walmart and Costco compete on price, not on services. When companies compete on price, and not on services, there is a high chance that there exists a gap-service need-that is not being satisfied. The gap represents an unfilled demand, underserved, or poorly served market, including a geographic market or market whose particular need is not addressed. These gaps are often found by an entrepreneur's own frustration about not being able to find a particular thing, being dissatisfied by an experience, or missing a particular function when doing something.

BIG PROBLEMS
— CREATE —
BIG OPPORTUNITIES

Example: Daisy Rock

The founder of Daisy Rock recognized that guitar manufacturers were creating and selling guitars predominantly geared toward the male population. The need of female guitar player was not being met, so Daisy Rock decided to sell guitars for women, incorporating design features that accommodate a woman's smaller hand and build.

Example: Casual Male

CASUAL|MALEXL   Casual Male is the typical "big & tall" clothing store, addressing the need of "big & tall" individuals that are not addressed in other stores.

Techniques for Generating Ideas and Opportunities

The vast majority of good ideas come from things that people have knowledge about, for example from their dissatisfaction as a customer, working within a particular industry, trying to solve a problem that they currently face, and hearing about problems from friends, family, and other industry contacts.

Every problem represents an opportunity for a creative solution. The entrepreneurial challenge is picking the right problems to solve. Additionally, while for every problem there is a creative solution, and in every solution resides an opportunity, not every solution represents a viable business concept.

One way to quickly distinguish between ideas and a real business concept could be to ask the following questions:

- Is there really a customer problem here?

- Will people actually pay to help solve this problem?

- Is the solution something that can be done in a reasonable way (time, money, etc.)?

- Does your solution truly create customer value?

To answer these questions more effectively, do a feasibility study of your idea and opportunity. There are several techniques that entrepreneurs can use in this process of concept generation, which include brainstorming, focus groups, surveys, and others.

BRAINSTORMING

One way to generate some quick ideas is a brainstorming session. This is an idea generating technique, not an idea analysis technique or tool.

Brainstorming can be an effective way to generate lots of ideas on a specific issue and then determine which idea (or ideas) is the best solution. Brainstorming is most effective with groups of 8-12 people with different backgrounds, and should be performed in a relaxed environment. If participants feel free to relax and joke around, they'll stretch their minds further and produce more creative ideas.

There are many approaches to brainstorming sessions and we will focus on the traditional approach, which has been the most effective at this stage of opportunity recognition.

As an entrepreneur, you will want to follow these **10 easy steps for an effective brainstorming session:**

1 Be the leader of the brainstorming session.

2 The brainstorming session should be in a relaxed environment and the facilitators should be equipped with a notepad or flip chart to write down the ideas.

3 Clearly define your problem or issue. A poorly designed challenge will produce poor results. A challenge that is clearly designed will produce a lot of excitement and many useful solutions and opportunities.

4 Have a time limit. Most experts recommend 25-30 minutes; however, this might depend on the size of the group and the nature of the challenge.

5 Before the session starts make it clear that there must be absolutely no criticizing of ideas. No matter how silly, how impossible, or how stupid an idea is or might sound, it must be considered and written down. Laughing is to be encouraged. Criticism is not encouraged nor allowed.

6 Once the brainstorming starts, participants should shout out solutions to the problem while the facilitator writes them down for all to see.

7 When the time is up, the entrepreneur should select five ideas which he/she likes best, or finds favorable, and everyone involved in the brainstorming session should be in agreement.

8 Write down about five criteria for judging which ideas best solve your problem. Criteria should start with the word "should," for example: "it should be cost effective," "it should be scalable," "it should be completed before January 1," and so on.

9 Give each idea a score of 0 to 5 points, depending on how well it meets each criterion. Once all of the ideas have been scored for each criterion, add up the scores.

10 The idea with the highest score will best solve your problem. But you should keep a record of all of your best ideas and their scores, in case your best idea does not turn out to be a great opportunity, or you could incorporate other ideas within your opportunity.

One of the key benefits of brainstorming is that it provides the entrepreneur with ideas that he/she would not have access to or hear from the same group in a more traditional setting. Since criticism is not allowed, everyone shares what is on their mind, even if it might be considered foolish. This setting allows and encourages innovation and creativity, while at the same time discourages evaluation of the proposed idea.

FOCUS GROUPS

A focus group is a way to reach out to your potential users for feedback and comment. Focus groups help answer questions that the entrepreneur cannot resolve and can lead to new ideas. A typical focus group consists of 5 to 10 people who are selected because of their relationship to the issue being discussed. Although focus groups are used for a variety of purposes, they can be used to help generate new business ideas.

Specifically, the **focus group session concentrates on:**

- Gathering opinions, beliefs, and attitudes about issues of interest to an entrepreneur's idea or business concept.

- Testing entrepreneur's assumptions.

- Encouraging discussion about a particular topic.

- Building excitement from spontaneous combination of participants' comments.

- Providing an opportunity to learn more about a topic or issue.

Focus groups help entrepreneurs uncover what's on the customers' minds through the give-and-take nature of a group discussion, however, the feedback does not necessarily represent how other customer segment(s) might think or feel. Just as in brainstorming sessions, the focus group should have underlying objective and goals, and utilize an experienced moderator to keep the group focused on the issue in question. **Below is an example of how the focus group can be used:**

An entrepreneur is thinking of developing an application for the restaurant chain ABC to help restaurant patrons reserve and pre-order their meals before they arrive. The entrepreneur might consider inviting 5-10 regular ABC restaurant patrons to participate in a focus group discussion and ask the group about their wait time, to first understand if the wait time is a problem for these focus group participants, in addition to asking if they own and use a smart phone. If wait time is a problem, and the focus group participants use smart phones, then the moderator would then present the idea/solution and ask for their opinions about the idea. The moderator would also use this opportunity to ask about potential features and benefits that they would like to see within that application. If 3-5 of the participants are smart phone users, the entrepreneur could identify some key features and benefits of the new application. Finally, the moderator could ask these 3-5 participants if they would use the application and even test the price they would pay.

SURVEYS

Surveys are another method of how an entrepreneur can collect customers' opinions about an idea and product or service. Surveys are generally used to draw conclusions or -test a specific idea or hypothesis. Surveys use random sampling techniques in order to infer from the sample to the population, the more people surveyed the better and more accurate the results will be. Surveys can be conducted over the telephone, by mail, online, or in-person. In terms of effectiveness, in-person is best, followed by telephone, mail, and online. However, the effect on cost and time is rather the opposite.

> ■ **SURVEYS** ■
> Do not use 'yes' or 'no' questions, since most customer decisions are not black-and-white.

When conducting surveys, the entrepreneur should include demographic questions, such as age, gender, and income, which will help to ensure that the correct customer is targeted.

Additionally, do not use 'yes' or 'no' questions, since most customer decisions are not black-and-white, rather include questions that require the survey-taker to scale an issue between 1 and 5, **for example:**

HOW SATISFIED ARE YOU WITH YOUR CABLE PROVIDER?				
1	2	3	4	5
(not satisfied at all)				(extremely satisfied)

Another type of question that the survey should contain is about attributes, **for example**:

HOW IMPORTANT ARE THE FOLLOWING CRITERIA TO YOUR SATISFACTION WITH YOUR CABLE PROVIDER?					
	Not at all				Extremely
Answers the phone quickly	1	2	3	4	5
Prompt repair service	1	2	3	4	5
Service never goes dark	1	2	3	4	5
Channel selection	1	2	3	4	5
Price	1	2	3	4	5

Finally, since you are testing if these customers will be purchasing your products or services, make sure to also include a question about intent to purchase, **for example**:

HOW LIKELY ARE YOU TO SIGN UP FOR THE NEW SUPERSTAR CHANNEL FOR AN EXTRA $12.99 A MONTH?				
Definitely	Probably	Might or might not	Probably not	Definitely not
(not satisfied at all)				(extremely satisfied)

An affordable tool for doing an online survey is Survey Monkey, *surveymonkey.com*, which costs approximately $20 per month, and for a limited number of questions is free.

OTHERS

Different entrepreneurs use different methods of generating ideas. Some additional ways to generate ideas include mentors, boards of advisors, competition mapping, and trade associations and peer review.

A mentor is someone who serves as an example, an advisor, sounding boards and ultimately a friend. That last attribute—a friend—is very important. A mentor cannot really be effective if he/she doesn't truly care for you, and vice versa. They don't work with aspiring entrepreneurs to make money or for promotional reasons. A mentor's main motivation in this relationship is to help other entrepreneurs succeed. When identifying a mentor, bear in mind that this should be an experienced businessperson who has great understanding of all business aspects, customers, and relationships within your industry. Ask your mentor to lunch, or just meet him/her for coffee for 30 minutes, and pick their brain about your idea, seek suggestions, advice, and resources such as contact info of experts within the filed or trade to do further research.

Boards of advisors are a small group of people who meet periodically to offer advice and direction to a company. Members of the board of advisors should be experienced business professionals and entrepreneurs. Entrepreneurs use boards of advisors for idea generation, feedback, and guidance, which will help them to get a foot in the market. Usually members of the board of advisors are not shareholders of the company and bare no legal responsibility of the decision making.

A competition map helps you see what competitors are doing and offering in a market. You can draw such a map quickly and objectively, it should be a matrix containing your potential competitors. Creating a competition map involves three steps. First, identify your market and consider all companies that your market will buy from. Second, track what your competitors offer to their customers, what are the main benefits, for example identify product variety, price, delivery, quality, warranty, and so on.

Competition maps help you see what competitors are doing and offering in a market.

For example, if you are planning to open a healthy deli in your town, some of the variables you want to look at are: what kind of sandwiches are offered, what are the prices, do they offer soups, number of people within 1 mile radius, healthy choices, parking, cleanliness, waiting lines, waiting times during peak hours, and so on. Third, draw the matrix, select rating scheme for the variables, and populate the matrix for each competitor.

What you get is a picture of the competitive landscape of your market, where you will be able to identify some gaps, some services or products that are not being offered or are not creating value to the customers, these gaps will provide some opportunities and help you come up with some new ideas for your business.

DELI COMPETITORS MAPPING - SAMPLEVILLE, NY			
	JOE'S DELICIOUS	MAIN STREET SANDWICHES & COFFEE	MAMA SUE'S DELI
Type of Sandwiches	Subs, panini	Subs	Subs
Healthy Choices	Whole wheat bread	Whole wheat bread & chips	Whole wheat bread
Organic/All Natural Food	No	Yes	No
Type of Organic/ All Natural Food	N/A	Apples & chips (all natural)	N/A
All Natural Soups	No	No	No
Delivery	No	No	No

The gaps that this map identifies include lack of organic sandwiches, healthy choices are limited, no organic or all natural soups are served, and none of the delis provides delivery services—some ideas that could be generated from this include organic wraps and sandwiches with all natural cheese, deli meat, and organic vegetables (tomatoes, lettuce, etc.), optional organic soup as side dish, and delivery services in a hybrid car.

Finally, trade associations and peer review could help generate some additional ideas. Some entrepreneurs attend trade shows, conferences, and other events of industry personnel with the goal to find out what the trends are, what the competition is doing, and then use that information to generate new ideas for products and/or services.

Will the Fish Bite - Conducting Feasability Analysis

Once you have identified an idea for a business opportunity, you need to know if this is also a profitable business opportunity, does it have a feasible market—will enough customers buy and use your products and services to allow your company to become a sustainable and profitable business.

CONDUCTING MARKET RESEARCH

Market feasibility research and analysis is an assessment of the overall appeal of the market for the product or service being proposed. Conducting market feasibility can provide a "reality check" of your business idea and help you define product/service development to ensure it is appealing for your customers. This type of research is used to determine:

- What is the demand for the product or service that an entrepreneur is considering to offer?

- What are potential customers' needs and price expectations of the products/services?

- What is the nature of the competitive space and the competition?

- What are the strengths and weaknesses of your competitors from your potential customers' perspective?

- What will it take for your potential customers to buy your products/services and keep them coming back for more?

In order to get these questions answered, a comprehensive market feasibility analysis includes an industry analysis, current market analysis, competition analysis, anticipated future market potential, and potential buyers and sources of revenue.

Industry analysis provides the big picture of the environment in which your business will be active. The first sign of feasibility is the growth stage of the industry; if the industry is growing it might be a good indicator for your business. Example: the smart phone industry is young and growing, and there are many opportunities for new companies to enter. While other industries, such as the internet search engine industry, are old and stagnated, with only few dominating key players and not much room for new entries. Furthermore, the number of companies within the industry is another indicator, for example if there are a high number of companies within an industry, chances are that the competition is intense and that they compete mostly on price.

In order to do the adequate research and find out about industry's growth stage and overall attractiveness, entrepreneurs need to do primary and secondary research. Primary research is research that is original and is collected by the entrepreneur. Primary research is done in the form of an interview, focus group, observation, and surveys. Secondary research includes the research of already collected data, such as industry reports, government reports, trade journal articles, scholarly articles, competitors' reports, and other source of data that one can find online and in public or private (university) libraries. Most libraries have a librarian who can help find these data bases that contain industry and market data and reports; hence, it is highly recommended that entrepreneurs reach out to their local libraries for assistance.

Once the primary and secondary research has been completed, the entrepreneur should have a clear understanding of the industry growth, including the key players, industry trends, and actual numbers of the industry/market size.

Current market analysis leverages the industry analysis in terms of understanding the big picture and trends within the industry, to narrow down analysis of a particular market within the industry, for example looking at the market within a particular industry in the five boroughs of New York City, or looking at the single moms market in the Northeast.

Just as in industry analysis, the primary and secondary research tools are being used. The research should help you understand the needs of the customers, understand their preferences, how they usually make a decision about purchasing particular products or services, and understand how much are they willing and able to pay for products/services. Finally, the current market analysis will help you understand if there are enough customers who are willing and able to purchase your products. This will help you understand who those customers are or could be, how many of them are there, which will help you understand this market size and market potential.

Competition analysis provides insights within the competitive space within your market. Primary and secondary research tools should be used in this analysis, too. The primary research can include: talking to suppliers to find out if there any exclusive agreements within the industry between them and your competitors, talking to competitors directly to find out what they charge for products/services, manufacturing or delivery capacities, and talking to existing customers to understand what the competition is doing, or not doing. The secondary data can include company reports that might be available on their websites, industry reports that provide information on the companies, and any public data that contains information about the company such as local newspaper articles. Developing a competitive map (see page 15) is highly recommend in order to have a better overview of the competitive filed, to understand the strengths and weaknesses of the competitors, while also being aware of opportunities that these could potentially create for you or any other new competitor.

Anticipated future market potential should be derived from the industry, market, and competition analyses. The industry growth will provide you indicators in terms of future trends, opportunities, and the growth rate, which entrepreneurs use to assess their growth rate and expansion. Further, the market research will indicate who the customer will be for your products/services and how many of them are willing and able to purchase and continue purchasing your products. And, finally, the competition analysis will help you understand the key players, their market shares, possible actions they will take once you enter the market, and provide you a realistic picture in terms of how much market you can capture. Tying these together will help you estimate the future market potential.

Potential buyers and sources of revenue will be evident through the market research. Most relevant data will come from the primary research, which will help understand the buyer's needs, pains, buying patterns, decision making choices, purchase frequency, willingness and ability to pay a certain price. Leveraging this data, you can think about diversifying your products and services, bundling products and services (for example, selling a product and including warranty options), selling only via an online store and the list goes on. This last piece of the market feasibility should provide you with a clear understanding of: what products/services you can sell, how much of it can you sell, how often you can sell it, what else you might need to sell/offer, how much you can charge, and what the revenues will be. This will help you understand the market and its potential and allow you to conduct financial feasibility analysis.

FINANCIAL FEASIBILITY

At this stage of idea generation, the financial feasibility analysis should be a rather simple one. A typical financial feasibility analysis includes: start-up capital requirements, start-up capital sources, and potential returns for investors.

Start-up capital requirement is an estimation of how much money you will need in order to start, run, and sustain your business for a year or two. Some of the start-up costs may include salaries, product development, website development, equipment, space, or facility, professional costs such as legal fees, marketing efforts, and other cost associated items and actions that will get the company to roll out the products/service and start generating income. At this stage, the start-up capital number should not be exact, but rather provide you with good understanding costs that will be inquired once the company is started.

Once you know how much start-up capital you will need; now, you need to find out what the **start-up capital source** could be and the **potential returns for investors** for each of these sources.

Once the start-up capital requirements are known, the entrepreneur will know if he/she will finance organically, out of pocket, or go to external resources. Most start-up companies are *self-financed*, this means that you use your savings and gumption to start and run the company until you make a profit that can be re-invested in the firm. This source of financing allows the entrepreneur to retain 100 percent ownership of the company.

In addition to self-financing, there are three external sources for raising capital: friends and family members, banks, and investors.

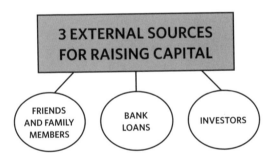

Friends and family members sometime people call this category the 3 F's: Family, Friends, and Fools. It is the second biggest source of funding. Asking for money is a sensitive issue, so try to ensure that this is set out in a formal way, where the risks and potential payout are explained. This can be worked out as a loan (debt) or as part of equity; however, it is in your best interest to try to retain as much control of the firm as possible. The potential returns for investors in this case will depend on your agreement with your investors, depending if it is a loan or equity.

Bank loans are another source of business capital. This is traditionally a good source of early stage funding for small businesses; however, it is difficult to get a bank loan for start-ups in the new economy. According to Pepperdine University, only 17% of loan-seeking small firms received bank funding in 2010. This type of financing is easier to get in the later stages of the firm. However, for small start-ups there are more readily available loans-micro-finance loans-which are usually offered at local community development organizations, such as community credit unions, which provide lines of credit between $5,000 and $20,000.

Keep in mind that the bank's goal is to make sure they get their money back with interest. They focus on risk reduction, to ensure that they get their money back. The banks will look at things like:

- What do you plan on doing with the money?

- How much do you need?

- When do you need it?

- How long will you need it?

- How will you repay the loan?

- What is the cash flow of the firm?

- What are the margins?

In addition to this, banks will look at the personal credit of the entrepreneur and the entrepreneur's character (which will include credit history, lawsuits, lines, background checks, and work experiences,) They want to know if times get tough, that the entrepreneur can convert other things into cash, in order to pay back the credit, and they want to know if he/she has personal assets (stocks, etc.) or business assets (inventory, equipment), which can be used as collateral. These issues will play a major role in the bank's decision. As such, there is a lot more focus on the entrepreneur's personal credit history and capacity to pay back the loan, rather than on the business idea itself and its potential.

Small Business Administration (SBA) Guaranteed Loans are another capital resource. The SBA has multiple programs to help finance start-ups and small firms and is the biggest small business backer in the nation. The SBA works with local banks to guarantee loans up to 75% (which may vary). These loans have good interest rates but require a personal guarantee, so the need for collateral still exists, although the collateral demands are somewhat lower than with traditional bank loans. The SBA also has a micro loan program for smaller loan amounts (under $50,000); and so far the average loan has been $13,000.

For more information about the variety of SBA loans, visit *sba.gov/content/sba-loans*, or talk to a resource partner about loan options.

Finally, the last source of funding is **professional investors: angel investors and venture capitalists.**

Angel investors are high net worth individuals, who usually have substantial industry and entrepreneurial experience themselves, and who are investing (equity) in relatively early stage ventures to help aspiring entrepreneurs financially and professionally by offering mentoring, coaching, and advising. These are the people who frequently want to give back (mentor, contribute to society) as well as make money and expect a decent return on investment—about 20-50% per year.

Even though **venture capitalists** do not typically invest in start-up companies, it is important that entrepreneurs know about them and how they finance businesses. Venture capitalists are professional investment companies that usually come in during growth stage, after the firm has achieved some sales and growth milestones. In terms of investments, they generally invest large amounts of money (over $500,000) for returns of a substantial amount of equity. Venture capitalists are looking for aggressive growth—home run hitters—and expect over 30% (often over 60%) return on investment per year.

The venture capitalists put controls in place to ensure returns, which oftentimes includes replacing the CEO or team members. In their due diligence, venture capitalists look for potential return, such as market size, market growth, competitors, lead time, and innovativeness of the idea, similar to the market analysis that we talked about previously in this chapter. They also look at the company's ability to ensure return and pay attention to the team experience, education, scope of market, intellectual property, and exit strategy.

Once you have identified a viable business opportunity, there are several entrepreneurial paths that you as an entrepreneur can pursue in exploiting this opportunity. These include starting a company from scratch, buying a franchise, buying an existing business, inheriting a business, or joining a start-up company.

CHAPTER 3

COMPARISON OF FUNDING SOURCES

	Self-Funded	Family & Friends	Bank/SBA	Angel	Venture Capitalist
Debt/Equity	Equity	Either	Debt	Equity	Equity
Need for Control	Retain all control	Maintain control	Maintain control	Give up some control	Give up control
Stage of Investment	At any stage	At any stage	Growth/Varies	Seed Stage	Growth Stages
Amount of $ Invested	Varies	Usually up to $100K	Varies	$25-500K	$500K+
Goals	Up to you	Depends	Get re-paid with interest	Growth, mentoring	High growth & make $$$
Biggest Advantage	Keep control	Relatively easy to get	Maintain control	Experience; good money	Amount of $$$ given; experience
Biggest Disadvantage	Limited amount of cash	Can lead to interpersonal issues	Need to make payments	Can lose control; demands vary	May lose control; high growth focus

Navigating Different Paths to Business Ownership

"Being an entrepreneur
means that I have the
ability to control my
destiny—to make a
difference in the world
in my own way."

Often people jump right to the assumption that becoming a business owner means starting a new company from nothing—creating something that 'didn't exist before in the world.' The reality is that there are many different paths to business ownership open to you, each with its own advantages and disadvantages. As such, choosing the path to business ownership that's right for you requires ample consideration. In this chapter, we will introduce five possible paths to business ownership:

1. Starting a new business

2. Buying an existing business

3. Purchasing a franchise

4. Inheriting a business (family business)

5. Joining an existing business as a partner, and/or being promoted by existing owners to be the professional manager and/or co-owner of an existing business

Each of these alternative paths to business ownership has advantages and disadvantages that we will discuss, in an effort to help you understand the alternative that best aligns with your personal goals and motivations.

Path #1: The Business "Start-Up"

To start a business from scratch requires that the entrepreneur identifies a market need and a unique way to satisfy that need, and then acts to plan and execute on the steps and stages related to launching a new venture.

Starting and building your own business has several advantages, including being your own boss. You begin fresh. You have total control of how the business will be managed. You are free from obligations to franchisors. Starting a business from scratch is the most risky path to business ownership; however, this path also represents a high potential for reward.

The downside of starting your own business is the work involved in the start-up process, including industry and market research, business plan, business licenses and permits, establishing credit lines with suppliers, and generating customers. New businesses often find it difficult to secure financing, and at the same time take longer to realize profit.

Tips on Starting a Business from Scratch

1 **Believe in yourself.** You need to convince yourself before you can convince others.

2 **Write and update a business plan.** Don't over-complicate your business plan. It should be easy to follow, easy to execute, and easy to modify. Clarity is more important than bulk. Use the plan as a compass to guide your business. Keep it clutter-free and keep it real.

3 **Surround yourself with great people.** You want people at your side who are responsible, accountable, and reliable. Look for people who complement you, compensate for your weakness, or offer a fresh perspective.

4 **Have a mentor.** You will need somebody who's been there and can provide you with perspectives that you are unable or unwilling to see. Mentors spare you from making costly mistakes or learning lessons the hard way.

5 **Stay focused and be consistent.** Focus on your business, do something sensational, and keep doing it until people buy into it. Be consistent, you'll get noticed and your business will turn into a reputable and reliable company.

6 **Stick to your strengths and core competencies.** If you are great at marketing snacks, why start selling computers? Stick to what you do best, to what you are most passionate about. Make the most of your company's core strengths.

7 **Take the long-term view of building your business.** Building a great, enduring business takes a lifetime. Make it your own. Enjoy every moment.

8 **Use common sense.** Mom always told you to use common sense. Why do it any differently now?

If you plan to start your own business, you will need to be prepared to dedicate significant time and energy, including working long days, with no days off, for an extended period of time while you focus on building your business.

ADVANTAGES OF START-UP BUSINESS

 There are numerous reasons that entrepreneurs and aspiring entrepreneurs choose to start a new business. We'll highlight just a few of those advantages:

■ **FREEDOM, AUTONOMY, & CONTROL:** You are the boss, and YOU control of all aspects of the business.

■ **NO HISTORY:** Start-up is new business, it does not have baggage and has nothing to protect. There are no employee problems, no supplier and/or customer challenges, no lawsuits, debts, or legal issues. In a start-up, you are completely untethered from these kinds of restrictions. Furthermore, you can dream up innovative ideas, without any regard to protecting the company's revenues/ employees/customers, or upsetting the politics of the organization. You are free to think of the way things should be if you could design the perfect world. You have freedom to try to disrupt the status quo.

■ **SPEED & AGILITY:** Big companies can't move as fast as you can. This is by far the most important advantage for a start-up. You may have a great idea, but I'll bet that the same idea is kicking around the big company competitor, too. The issue for them is that they have a huge organization to drag behind them. They can't turn on a dime; they can't make fast decisions, i.e. implementation and use of new technology. You can. You can get there first. And getting there first is huge.

■ **A DIFFERENT KIND OF EMPLOYEE.** There are lots of really, really smart people that work for big organizations. But there is something that brings the best out in people when they work in a start-up. The start-up environment is so empowering and invigorating when you realize that you have a HUGE impact on the success or failure of your company. It's on you. You have the power to change a market, and you get caught up in the journey and the mission. Small start-ups can accomplish amazing things.

■ **LIFE STYLE:** Entrepreneurs usually start businesses doing something they love. Growing a business from a hobby or part-time job gives entrepreneurs a chance to improve their lives because they are working in an environment important to them. Working in a positive business

CHAPTER 4

environment may not really seem like work to an entrepreneur.

DISADVANTAGES OF START-UP BUSINESS

While there are several advantages to incorporating a small business, there are also challenges that should be considered:

RISK: Start-up businesses are typically more costly and risky since there is no proven formula. Start-up businesses have high risk of failure in the first two years of operation.

NO NAME RECOGNITION: If you start a business, you have no history. Everything must be generated from scratch, including developing name recognition; whereas an existing business or franchise has a recognizable name and brand, which can guarantee immediate acceptance of the businesses within the new market.

CASH FLOW: Start-up businesses may not have a positive cash flow for two to three years. Hence, your new start-up may require your own capital to operate the business. Being a new business, you may not be able to get credit from the bank, so you may need to borrow money from family, friends, and use your credit cards. Sometimes it takes up to two or three years to establish credit with a lending institution and suppliers. On the other hand, established businesses or franchises provide access to immediate cash flow.

MARRIED TO THE BUSINESS: This is a common phrase from small business owners. It basically means that your hours of work and level of commitment is such that you cannot take a holiday, your business is always with you (days, nights, and weekends) and basically, your neck is on the line. You can't just throw the keys back and give it all away if it gets too hard.

RESOURCES: Start-up businesses may not have many resources besides money; they may lack experienced employees. Established businesses and franchises provide these resources, since they usually come with the support of experienced workers, training, and management support. As such, one of the greatest challenges related to starting an entirely new venture is finding people with the 'right' set of skills and expertise to support your efforts.

MITIGATING THE RISK OF BUSINESS START-UP

In order to start your own business, and make it grow to be a successful stream of income, there are many things to consider and be prepared for beforehand. Doing business, which is your passion, is the first thing to consider as success. A feeling of fulfillment is a lot better when you were able to make a small business grow, and at the same time, it is something that you really wanted in the first place.

The following **recommendations** are essential **for successful business start-up** and **risk mitigation**:

◼ The first recommendation is to develop a clear short- and long-term **vision** for your business. Your vision will give you purpose, will help you keep focused on what you want the business to achieve. Your vision will help your clients understand what you and your business stand for, and keep your employees and investors, if any, focused on your goals.

◼ Write a **business plan** and update on a regular basis. You have heard the proverb: "Those who fail to plan, plan to fail." You have a passion, and you'd like to make it your profession. No matter how enthusiastic you are about your small business, though, it won't be successful unless you have a plan in place for how you're going to start and run it. The business plan should be the road map for your business, and even though the outcomes will be different, at least you will be aware and prepared for the unexpected. Dwight Eisenhower once said, "I have always found that plans are useless, but planning is indispensable." It doesn't matter how long or detailed your plan is, as long as it covers the essential points. Most successful small businesses will need to have a clear market understanding, operations, break-even analysis, a profit-loss forecast, and a cash-flow analysis. A business plan is essential because it allows you to experiment with the strategy for your business on paper; therefore, it is important to be realistic when writing the business plan.

◼ Hire the best **people**, and manage them well. As your business grows, you will be faced with the enormous task of hiring and managing other people. The quality of your people is the key to your success. Find people who share your passion and vision for what you want to accomplish with the business. Then work hard to keep your good people. Invest in your people, and they will appreciate working for your business.

◼ **Differentiate** your business through your concept or presentation. Your business is unique. Even if you offer the same products, clearly define your unique selling proposition, to help users see your business apart from your competitors.

◼ Leverage existing **resources for entrepreneurs**, for example, resources offered by the SBA (*www.sba.gov*), such as business counseling, mentoring, and financing. You will need somebody who's been there and can provide you with perspectives that you are unable or unwilling to see; in this case, business counselors, mentors, and coaches will spare you from making costly mistakes or learning lessons the hard way. Another great resource for entrepreneurs are business incubators, which offer an entrepreneurial atmosphere and culture, where entrepreneurs are surrounded by other entrepreneurs, mentors, innovators, and other like-minded individuals.

■ Keep your **focus**. It is important to identify and concentrate on making the unique aspects of your business as superb as possible. Every day, your focus should be on how to further enhance your business. Profit is, after all, the ultimate goal of any successful small business. You should examine your business' expenses (rent, materials, employee compensation, etc.) and then figure out how much you will need to sell to cover those costs and start generating a profit. This is known as a break-even analysis.

■ Protect yourself. Identify and hire your **BAIL** (Banker, Accountant, Insurance, Lawyer) team, consult with them on what business entity best fits your needs, what is the right insurance you must and should have, what certifications and permits your business needs, how to protect your intellectual property, and anything else that has to do with legal, liability, and tax issues.

■ Keep your edge. There are many ways to gain a **competitive edge** over other businesses in your industry: you could have a better product, a more efficient manufacturing or distribution process, a more convenient location, better customer service, or a better understanding of the changing marketplace. Identify your competitive edge and be consistent. Consistency will reinforce your competitive edge and establish your reputation of being a dependable and reliable business. Another way to hold onto your competitive edge is to stay proactive. If you know that your business is going to face challenges or encroachment by a competitor, don't wait to react--plan ahead and you'll stay ahead.

■ **Pay your bills and taxes on time**. To avoid any harsh penalties from the IRS, or even jeopardize your personal assets, remit payroll and sales taxes on time. Furthermore, pay your suppliers on time, do not burn bridges with them, it will have a negative impact on your business relationship and will cause hindrances to establishing revolving credit. Plus, if you stay current on your debts and pay them as you incur them, it will help you avoid being overwhelmed by cash flow problems if several debts come due simultaneously.

Path #2: Buying an Existing Business

Purchasing an existing business represents another viable path to business ownership. Many concepts or ideas fit within established business models, which offer the benefits of existing customers, and hopefully a positive reputation. Buying an existing business has numerous advantages over creating a business from scratch; however, there are also risks associated with this path. We'll briefly highlight both.

ADVANTAGES OF BUYING AN EXISTING BUSINESS

 There are several advantages of buying an existing business:

■ Buying an existing business reduces the time and energy expended in establishing a new business.

■ The company has already been formed, employees are in place, relationships with vendors established, and the business has regular customers. Established customers provide immediate sales and cash flow, which also demonstrates that there is proven demand for the product or services that the business offers.

■ Provided the business you buy has been profitable and has a good track record, establishing financing to build or expand the business will be less challenging.

■ The investment when purchasing existing businesses is usually less than the one for starting a new company, and often times the owner of the company provides financing that will allow you to purchase the business.

■ Many of the problems will have been discovered and solved already.

DISADVANTAGES OF BUYING AN EXISTING BUSINESS

■ Some of the disadvantages of buying an existing business are:

■ Identifying the right business that fits your needs, experience, and financial capacity might be challenging and time-consuming.

■ It is difficult to estimate the value of the business. You often need to invest a large amount up front, and will also have to budget for professional fees for solicitors, surveyors, accountants, etc. Furthermore, if the business has been neglected you may need to invest quite a bit more on top of the purchase price to give it the best chance of success.

■ You may need to honor or renegotiate any outstanding contracts the previous owner leaves in place.

■ You may encounter staff problems. Staff members often leave their jobs when a new operator takes over the business, especially when they dislike the change, while some leave with staff entitlements, such as severance pay.

■ The business may have a bad reputation that is very difficult to overcome.

■ The lease agreement may be a problem due to the relationship of the landlord and the previous owner.

■ The premises may be very small and hamper future growth.

TIPS FOR BUYING AN EXISTING BUSINESS

Buying a business that is already operating is an excellent way to get started and has many advantages. But, as with any business decision, your purchase takes careful thought and research. The first step is to determine what type of business to buy. This could depend on your personal interests, previous work experience, life style, or a number of other criteria. Make sure that your prospective business fits your needs.

After deciding on the business type, you need to locate a business for sale. You can contact businesses yourself, look in newspaper advertisements, ask friends or acquaintances for suggestions, or get professional help from a real estate broker or consultant.

When you find a business that you are interested in, plan to do some serious research and analysis. You need to study the records, ask questions of customers and neighbors, do market research, and learn all that you can about the business. Professionals will be very helpful at this time, especially an accountant and lawyer. Some of the areas to evaluate include:

■ Location

■ Physical assets, such as equipment, fixtures, inventory

■ Personnel

■ Client base and customer loyalty

■ Financial condition

■ Products or services offered

- Warranty liabilities

- Business relationships with sup
pliers, distributors, etc.

Once you have evaluated these areas, the next question you are faced with is: How much is the business worth? There is really no simple answer to this question. The fair market value comes down to what the buyer is willing to pay and the seller is willing to accept. A dollar value for a business can be derived in several ways. One is to look at replacement cost; what it would cost to start the business from scratch. Some parts of a business are easy to calculate: inventory, equipment, fixtures, etc. But others are more difficult to put a dollar value on, such as customer base, name recognition, and goodwill. Another approach looks at the return on investment. For example, if you expect a 25 percent annual return from your business, you can look at the net cash flow of the prospective business and calculate what it is worth. Many business brokers use an income multiplier, that is, an accepted industry factor which is multiplied by the annual gross income of the business. Another easy approach is to compare with other similar businesses on the market. Professional appraisers may be able to provide a dollar value for businesses.

Checklist for buying an existing business

- The reason for the sale of the business.

- A report on whether the business fits your needs, experience, and financial capacity.

- A checklist on the operations of the business, including sales, profit and loss, and assets.

- Research on current and potential competitors.

- Check on the contracts for current and future deals with the customers.

- A review of the draft agreement with a lawyer.

Now it's time to prepare a purchase offer. This is an opportunity to work with the seller to negotiate the best solutions for both of you. Some **common types of business transactions** are:

- **Outright purchase.** The disadvantage of this is that it leaves the seller with little incentive to be concerned with your success as a new owner. If you find a problem, you may have difficulty recovering any money.

- **Phased-in purchase.** The buyer acquires the business over a period of time, usually three to five years.

- **Lease management.** The business is leased from the owner for a period of time, with the option to purchase at a later date for a specified price and terms.

■ **Marketing agreement.** This is a long-term contract that gives you exclusive rights to market a product within a particular area without buying the entire company.

■ **Licensing contract.** An alternative to purchase, in which your product is manufactured and distributed by an existing company.

■ **Management contract.** You manage the business for a fee with the option to buy if the business meets your expectations. As with all business transactions, the terms need to be carefully spelled out.

There are many ways to finance a business purchase. Each has its own benefits and risks. Creativity can be exercised to come up with the best solution for both buyer and seller. Preparing the purchase offer and closing the sale should be handled with the assistance of your lawyer. Be familiar with the terms of the agreements and the legal documents involved.

Path #3: Franchising

A franchise represents a type of business model where the franchise owner sells the rights to their business logo and model to third parties, called franchisees (YOU). Franchises are an extremely common way of becoming a business owner. In fact, it's difficult to drive more than a few blocks in most cities without seeing a franchise business. Examples of well-known franchise business models include McDonalds, 7-11, Subway, UPS Stores, and H & R Block. In the United States, there are franchise business opportunities available across a wide variety of industries, and there are also special programs to help military veterans pursue franchise opportunities (See Chapter 5).

To become a franchisee, you must first pay an initial fee for the rights to the business, and also invest in the required training and the equipment specified by that particular franchise owner. Thereafter, the franchisee will generally pay the franchise business owner an ongoing royalty payment, either on a monthly or quarterly basis. This payment is usually calculated as a percentage of the franchise operation's gross sales.

After the franchise agreement is completed and the franchisee has completed the required training, the franchisee will launch what is essentially a "replica" of the franchise business, under the direction of the franchise owner. The franchisee does not have as much control over business operations as compared to a situation where the business is a new venture. For example, the franchiser owner will require that the franchisee conforms to a very specific business model; the franchiser owner will require the franchisee to use the uniforms, business methods, and signs or logos dictated in the franchise agreement. Further, the franchisee will generally have to conform to national pricing models so as to maintain consistency with national advertising campaigns.

So while the franchisee is an independent owner of a given franchise location, the business model and certain operational details will be determined by the franchise owner. The trade-off is that the franchisee is positioned to realize the benefits of investing in an already-established brand and reputation. That is, the franchisee is not just buying the right to sell the franchisers product, but is also investing in the right to leverage a successful and tested business process.

ADVANTAGES OF OWNING A FRANCHISE

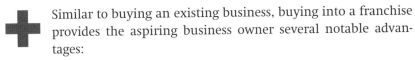 Similar to buying an existing business, buying into a franchise provides the aspiring business owner several notable advantages:

■ Purchasing a franchise, the franchisee enjoys the benefits of a startup and the benefits of buying an existing business.

■ Franchisees have an 80 percent chance of surviving.

■ Franchisee is buying an already proven working business model with infrastructure already in place and an established brand recognition and promotional strategy. For example, McDonalds is a very well-known name and they attract a lot of customers.

■ Many franchisors offer assistance in marketing and management support. Some even assist in securing the financing to franchisees, while some are able to get their own.

■ Lenders and banks are more willing to extend credit to franchisees as they face less risk than those who start their own businesses.

DISADVANTAGES OF OWNING A FRANCHISE

While there are many benefits to investing in an already-successful franchise business model, there are drawbacks as well:

■ Some of disadvantages include the high franchise fees required upfront. These fees can range from a couple thousand dollars to hundreds of thousands, depending on the franchise. Some franchises do not offer the support and assistance to help new franchisees get started.

■ Buying into well-known franchises is very expensive. If this is your choice, you will have to have extremely deep pockets or the ability to arrange the necessary financing.

■ You are limited and bound to the contract to which you have to adhere, so in many cases there is not much room for uniqueness, innovation, and growth.

■ Not all franchisors offer the same degree of assistance in starting a business and operating it successfully. Some are just start-up operations – and everything after start-up is up to you. Others make promises of ongoing training and support that they don't follow-up on.

■ Buying a little-known, perhaps inexpensive franchise can be a real gamble. Just because a business is offering franchises is no guarantee that the franchise you buy will be successful. In some cases, franchising is the business; all the franchisor is interested in is selling more franchises. Whether or not the individual franchises are successful is irrelevant to them. This is not to say that no little known, inexpensive franchises are worthwhile, but just a reminder that any franchise you're thinking of buying needs to be investigated carefully.

BECOMING A FRANCHISEE

Buying a franchise is like buying any other kind of business in that you have to do your due diligence and investigate the franchise fully. However, if you are the right sort of person for a franchise operation and pick the right franchise, being a franchisee can indeed be the fast track to success.

As with any investment you make, you should do your research thoroughly before you make any franchise purchasing decisions. Research the franchise, talk to other franchisees in the business, and check to see if they have a good support team for new franchisees. See how successful others are and if they are happy; ask a lot of questions. Visit a franchise unit and spend some time there. Talk to the owner and customers. Imagine working there for years and reflect if it fits your personal interests and needs.

When you find a franchise you like, contact the franchisor to request information. Generally, you will be asked to provide some basic information, including personal financial data. If this initial paperwork is satisfactory, you should be invited to visit the home office where you will usually receive a tour, sales presentation, and a Uniform Offering Circular (UFOC) with information about the company. This information should help in your decision to negotiate a franchise purchase.

Study the UFOC carefully. It is highly recommended that you contact an experienced franchise attorney for further assistance in analyzing the financial statements, litigation history, and other background information. Examine the franchise agreement carefully with the lawyer. Talk to as many franchisees and visit as many units as possible. Proceed with the deal only when you are fully satisfied that this is the business for you.

VetFran

VetFran, an International Franchise Association (IFA) program, helps returning service members access franchise opportunities through training, financial assistance, and industry support.

VetFran includes more than 400 IFA franchisor member companies offering financial incentives, training and mentoring to veterans interested in a career path in franchising. VetFran is unique because it provides financial incentives not otherwise available to other franchise investors. Since the program's inception in 1991, more than 2,100 veterans have become franchise business owners through VetFran.

Franchise ownership allows veterans to be in business for themselves, but not by themselves. There are many benefits and reasons why owning a franchise makes sense for veterans:

■ Franchises run on systems, just like the military. Implementing systems is a key responsibility in the military, and that aspect translates to the franchise world.

Support for Veteran Franchise Ownership: "Help Veterans Own Franchises Act"

The Help Veterans Own Franchises (HVOF) Act, sponsored by Sen. Bob Casey (D-Pa.) and Rep. Aaron Schock (R-Ill.), establishes a tax credit for honorably discharged veterans to become small business owners by offering tax credits to offset start-up costs equal to 25% of franchise fees. The legislation is part of a bipartisan jobs bill co-sponsored by Sens. Marco Rubio (R-Fla.) and Christopher Coons (D-Del.) and U.S. Reps. Richard Hanna (R-NY) and Bill Keating (D-Mass.) called the AGREE Act.

■ Franchises offer support. By joining a franchise you are surrounded by a support structure and are part of a franchise "family"—a culture many franchisors work to cultivate among their franchisees.

To learn more about the participating 400 franchises and the incentives they provide, visit *http://www.franchise.org/Veteran-Franchise.aspx.*

CHAPTER 4

Path #4: Inherit or Assume Management of a Family Business

Inheritance of a business is not restricted to parent-child or grandparent-grandchild; it can be passed down to nieces, nephews, cousins, or even in-laws. Inheriting a business, more often than not, comes with its own baggage; however, the advantage of inheritance is that you avoid a lot of the start-up efforts that are needed to establish a profitable business with products and customers.

Transition process is one of the most crucial steps in business inheritance. Inheriting a business can put a great deal of pressure on a newcomer; expectations are high, the standards to be lived up to are even higher.

But the real challenge comes when change needs to be effected, much of which might not go down well with a team all too comfortable with the existing way of doing things.

Entrepreneurs who are thinking about inheriting a business from a family member should first do some soul searching to find out if they are interested in taking up the new responsibility, evaluate whether the business is built on values, ideas, and principles that they agree with, and discuss it with those involved.

> **Entrepreneurs who are thinking about inheriting a business from a family member** should find out if the business is built on values, ideas and principles that they agree with.

Introducing changes and overcoming issues in the management style at work will become much simpler once you have a clear idea of what you would like to keep untouched.

Path #5: Join Existing Business as Professional Manager or Co-Owner

If you're not quite ready to start your own business, either from scratch or buying an existing one, you can start out by working in a start-up as a professional manager or co-owner. Getting in on the ground floor of a start-up business can be quite a rewarding experience. Just as start-up entrepreneurs must be risk takers, start-up employees must be willing to put in long hours and must accept the reality that if the start-up fails, they'll be out of a job. As was the case with the other paths to business ownership that we have described, this path has its own advantages and disadvantages.

ADVANTAGES OF JOINING A START-UP COMPANY

 There are several important and powerful advantages related to taking a position at a start-up company as a path to eventual business ownership:

■ Innovation is huge part of a start-up company; hence, as manager or co-owner, you become part of a team that is constantly striving to improve its product or service and other aspects of the company. Working for a start-up can be a roller-coaster ride, but if you love change and challenges, you're likely to thrive.

■ Start-ups attract innovative and visionary people who think creatively, differently, and progressively. If you crave a creative workplace with lots of collaboration and brainstorming, a start-up could be the place for you.

■ Start-ups offer opportunities to work with everyone involved with the company, including working directly with the CEO on a regular basis. This opportunity provides a strong sense of togetherness and purpose that larger, more hierarchical companies often lack.

■ Start-ups also offer opportunities to work on numerous projects, one day you are doing market research, the next day you are pitching to investors. These different projects and tasks provide opportunities for new skill development.

■ Just as starting a business from scratch, the risk of working for a start-up is high, as are the rewards if the business becomes successful. The advantage here is that you are part of a team that adds different values to the start-up, i.e. experiences, past business ownership, established networks, and more.

■ There are no predetermined formulas or rules to follow; much less restrictive than a franchise or business opportunity purchase.

■ Working in a start-up with huge growth potential can be very rewarding. As the start-up grows, employees who were in on the ground floor often advance quickly and have the chance to play leadership roles.

CHAPTER 4

DISADVANTAGES OF JOINING A START-UP COMPANY

There are also some notable disadvantages related to taking a position at a start-up company as a path to eventually becoming the 'boss' that include:

■ Being part of a start-up means being part of a team, so decision making is done by the team and/or the CEO. Due to the lack of hierarchy, it is important to get along with others within the company; otherwise it will be a painful and fruitless experience.

■ Start-up businesses are typically more costly and risky since there is no proven formula.

■ Too many start-ups fail not because of market forces, but because the founders simply could not agree on important issues.

Hopefully this chapter opened your eyes to the fact that becoming a business owner is not necessarily about simply starting a new company from nothing—creating something that 'didn't exist before in the world.' There are actually many different paths to business ownership open to you, each with its own advantages and its disadvantages. Think long and hard about the path to business ownership that's right, and make an informed choice.

Veteran Business Owner Profile

NAME: Kelly and Laura Broome

PROGRAM: Operation Endure & Grow, Syracuse University, Class of 2008

BRANCH: U.S. Army

BUSINESS: Franchise, ARCpoint Labs of San Antonio & ARCpoint Labs of Austin

Kelly and Laura Broome, co-owners of ARCpoint Labs of San Antonio and Austin, currently live in in San Antonio, with their sons James (27, serving in the U.S. Army Reserves), Gregory (15) and Justin (14).

Kelly served as a Civil Affairs officer while completing tours in Haiti and Bosnia, and more recently in both Afghanistan and Iraq. Following his time on active duty, he worked for eight years in defense contracting while continuing to serve as an Army Reserve officer. He has reached the rank of lieutenant colonel.

Though Kelly enjoyed consulting for Department of Defense (DOD) projects and facilitating the security of the nation, he was looking for a bigger challenge where he could directly manage the growth and development of an organization. He explored the possibility of owning his own business. Both Kelly and his wife, Laura, were looking for a company new to Texas in an emerging field. After years of traveling to combat zones, Kelly welcomed the idea of managing a company locally in Texas.

In June 2011, Kelly and Laura embarked on their journey by enrolling in the Institute for Veterans and Military Families' Operation Endure & Grow program, where they learned the basic skills and essentials necessary to start a business with a solid foundation. Just four months later, in October 2011, Kelly and Laura started their own business ARCpoint Labs of San Antonio. ARCpoint, a franchise, is a nationwide leader in drug, alcohol, DNA and background screening and has become one of the fastest growing third party providers in the industry. By opening a franchise, Kelly and Laura could follow the general blueprint the company laid out while maintaining the freedom and flexibility to make changes to fit the specific needs of their customers. Both Kelly and Laura find this particularly appealing, and have grown their venture into quite a success.

In February 2012, Kelly and Laura opened their second ARCpoint Labs, located in Austin. As they continue to expand, Kelly and Laura are eager for the opportunity to add more veterans and members of the Reserves to their growing staff.

CHAPTER 5

Services Supporting Veteran Business Ownership

"Entrepreneurship is freedom creating... entrepreneurship is the foundation of a democratic society."

A s you establish and grow your business, it is critical to identify resources that can benefit your business and allow you to be successful. You may want to access and use benefits and resources (information, funding, networks, access to employers, assistive technology, and others) in your community.

Why these resources may be important for you to consider:

■ If you need assistive technology to operate your business, or you think that any of your employees may have that need, there may be agencies that could pay for that equipment or worksite modifications.

■ If you intend to hire people with disabilities, some of these resources can help you leverage incentives such as On-the-Job Training Grants, subsidized wage or job coaching programs that your employees with disabilities can access.

■ Some of the resources may represent sources of capital for your business.

How to use this resource guide:

■ Explore the resources in the list below, either through web search or direct contact, to obtain more information on any that interest you.

CHAPTER 5

■ Incorporate any resources that fit within the Business Owner Profile and your Business Plan, for example, you may identify a need for start-up money and plan to apply to your State VR agency for a portion of that cost that you will include in your business financial projections.

Assistive Technologies

GRIFFIN-HAMMIS ASSOCIATES LLC

■ *http://www.griffinhammis.com/*

A full-service consultancy specializing in developing communities of economic cooperation and self-employment opportunities for people with disabilities, Griffin-Hammis serves people with disabilities by providing consultation in community rehabilitation improvement, job creation and job site training, employer development, self-employment feasibility and refinement, Social Security benefits analysis and work incentives, management-leadership mentoring, and civic entrepreneurship.

STATE ASSISTIVE TECHNOLOGY PROJECT (SATP)

■ *http://www.ataporg.org/*

With funding support from the federal government, each state operates an assistive technology project to assist individuals with disabilities access assistive technology devises needed to live and work independently. Your SATP can help you to identify technology options and link you to the resources available to acquire the technology.

Federal Resources

BETTER BUSINESS BUREAU (BBB)

■ *http://www.bbb.org*

BBB sees trust as a function of two primary factors — integrity and performance. Integrity includes respect, ethics and intent. Performance speaks to a business's track record of delivering results in accordance with BBB standards and/or addressing customer concerns in a timely, satisfactory manner. BBB ensures that high standards for trust are set and maintained. We exist so consumers and businesses alike have an unbiased source to guide them on matters of trust. We provide educational information and expert advice that is free of charge and easily accessible.

CHAPTER 5

CENTER FOR VETERANS ENTERPRISE

http://www.vetbiz.gov

The principal purposes of this site are to provide information about the VIP (Vendor Information Page) verification process; to assist veteran business owners in registering their business in the Secretary's Database of Veteran-owned small businesses and to enable VA contracting officers to easily identify service-disabled veteran-owned small businesses (SDVOSBs) and VOSBs eligible for procurement opportunities. Contact information: (email) verificationfollowup@va.gov; (phone) 202-303-3260.

CENTRAL CONTRACTOR REGISTRATION (CCR)

https://www.bpn.gov/ccr/default.aspx

CCR is the primary registrant database for the U.S. government, which collects, validates, stores, and disseminates data in support of agency acquisition missions.

CODE OF FEDERAL REGULATIONS (CFR)

http://www.gpoaccess.gov/cfr/

CFR is the codification of the general and permanent rules published in the federal register by the executive departments and agencies of the federal government. The online CFR is a joint project authorized by the National Archives and Records Administration's Office of the Federal Register and the Government Printing Office to provide the public with enhanced access to government information.

CONSUMER FINANCIAL PROTECTION BOARD (CFPD)

http://www.consumerfinance.gov

The CFPD is working to give consumers the information they need to understand the terms of their agreements with financial companies. We are working to make regulations and guidance as clear and streamlined as possible so providers of consumer financial products and services can follow the rules on their own.

DEPARTMENT OF LABOR (DOL)

http://www.dol.gov/

The DOL provides national policies, news, resources, laws and regulations in regard to all employment topics (i.e., hiring, disability resourc-

CHAPTER 5

es, health plans and benefits, veteran employment, retirement plans, benefits, and savings). Resources can be easily accessed by topic for the specific areas you may be interested in, such as disability resources and veterans employment (*http://www.dol.gov/dol/topic/*); by audience, such as people with disabilities, veterans, women *(http://www.dol.gov/dol/audience/)*; and by location, to find local and regional DOL programs (*http:// www.dol.gov/dol/location.htm*).

DEPARTMENT OF VETERANS AFFAIRS VETS SUCCESS PROGRAM (VR&E)

■ *http://www.vba.va.gov/bln/vre/def.htm#scd*

The mission of the VR&E program is to help veterans with service-connected disabilities to prepare for, find, andkeep suitable jobs. After eligibility is determined, Veterans are connected to a vocational rehabilitation counselor to assist with developing and pursuing educational and/or vocational goals. Counselors also provide services to veterans interested in self-employment.

■ For more information about the Veteran Entrepreneurship Program, go to *http://vetsuccess.gov/.*

■ You can review the Department of Veterans Affairs policy on vocation rehabilitation at *http://www.warms.vba.va.gov/M28_1.html.*

■ For more information about the VR & E program, go to *http://www. vba.va.gov/bln/vre/.*

■ To apply for VR&E services, go to *http://vabenefits.vba.va.gov/vonapp/ main.asp* or contact a nearby VA medical center or counseling office and inquire about vocational rehabilitation services.

■ Disabled Veterans Outreach Program (DVOP): *http://www.dol.gov/ vets/programs/fact/Employment_Services_fs01.htm*

The DOL operates the DVOP in conjunction with each state. DVOP specialists link veterans who have service-connected disabilities to job development and training opportunities. Most DVOP Specialists are located in One-Stops (see information about One-Stops in next section) while some are located in VA regional offices, medical centers or vet employment and training services.

FEDBIZOPPS

■ *http://www.fbo.gov*

This database houses federal government contracting opportunities, including notices of proposed government procurement actions and contract awards that serve as the single government point-of-entry for federal government procurement opportunities over $25,000.

FEDERAL DEPOSIT INSURANCE CORPORATION (FDIC)

■ *http://www.FDIC.gov*

The FDIC preserves and promotes public confidence in the U.S. financial system by insuring deposits in banks and thrift institutions for at least $250,000; by identifying, monitoring and addressing risks to the deposit insurance funds; and by limiting the effect on the economy and the financial system when a bank or thrift institution fails.

FEDERAL RESERVE BANK (FRB)

■ *http://www.federalreserveeducation.org*

The FRB supervises and regulates a wide range of financial institutions and activities. The Federal Reserve works in conjunction with other federal and state authorities to ensure that financial institutions safely manage their operations and provide fair and equitable services to consumers. Bank examiners also gather information on trends in the financial industry, which helps the Federal Reserve System meet its other responsibilities, including determining monetary policy.

FEDERAL TRADE COMMISSION (FTC)

■ *http://www.ftc.gov*

The FTC is the only federal agency with both consumer protection and competition jurisdiction in broad sectors of the economy. The FTC pursues vigorous and effective law enforcement; advances consumers' interests by sharing its expertise with federal and state legislatures and U.S. and international government agencies; develops policy and research tools through hearings, workshops, and conferences; and creates practical and plain-language educational programs for consumers and businesses in a global marketplace with constantly changing technologies. FTC's work is performed by the Bureaus of Consumer Protection, Competition and Economics.

CHAPTER 5

FINANCIAL LITERACY & EDUCATION COMMISSION (FLEC)

■ *http://www.MyMoney.gov*

All 22 Federal entities represented on this website work together on these issues as part of the FLEC that was created by Congress in 2003 through passage of the Financial Literacy and Education Improvement Act under Title V of the Fair and Accurate Credit Transactions Act of 2003 (P.L. 108-159). Congress designated the U.S. Department of Treasury's Office of Financial Education to lend its expertise and provide primary support to the FLEC, which is chaired by the Secretary of the U.S. Department of the Treasury and composed of 22 other Federal entities. The newly-created Consumer Financial Protection Bureau is also a member of FLEC.

With support from the Treasury Department's Office of Financial Education, the FLEC has worked with its member Federal agencies to improve financial literacy and education and provide free, reliable financial information to the American public through the *MyMoney.gov* Website, and the toll-free 1-888-MyMoney hotline.

FIRSTGOV

■ *http://www.firstgov.com*

FirstGov is a portal to access to all government and government agencies websites. It also contains resources and information regarding specific topics, such as jobs and education, health and nutrition, money and taxes.

GIVE ME 5

■ *http://www.giveme5.com/*

Program aimed at increasing the number of women receiving federal contracts through training, resources, events, and much more.

INTERNAL REVENUE SERVICE (IRS)

■ *http://IRS.gov*

The IRS provides America's taxpayers top quality service by helping them understand and meet their tax responsibilities and enforce the law with integrity and fairness to all.

This mission statement describes our role and the public's expectation about how we should perform that role.

- In the United States, the Congress passes tax laws and requires taxpayers to comply.

- The taxpayer's role is to understand and meet his or her tax obligations.

The IRS role is to help the large majority of compliant taxpayers with the tax law, while ensuring that the minority who are unwilling to comply pay their fair share. *http://www.irs.gov/businesses/small/index.html*

NATIONAL ASSOCIATION OF WOMEN BUSINESS OWNERS CENTER (NAWBO)

- *http://www.nawbo.org*

The NAWBO provides information, resources, and tools to support and promote economic development within the female entrepreneurial community. NAWBO also values diversity and represents the full diversity of the women business owner community.

NATIONAL FEDERATION OF INDEPENDENT BUSINESS (NFIB)

- *http://www.nfib.com/home*

The NFIB is the leading small business association representing small and independent businesses. This site gives NFIB members access to many business products and services at discounted costs. NFIB also provides timely information designed to help small businesses succeed.

NORTH AMERICAN INDUSTRY CLASSIFICATION SYSTEM (NAICS)

- *http://www.census.gov/eos/www/naics/index.html*

The NAICS is used by Federal statistical agencies in classifying business establishments for the purpose of collecting, analyzing, and publishing statistical data related to the U.S. business economy. This site provides the latest information on plans for NAICS revisions, as well as access to various NAICS reference files and tools.

U.S. SECURITIES AND EXCHANGE COMMISSION (SEC)

- *http://www.sec.gov*

The mission of the SEC is to protect investors, maintain fair, orderly, and efficient markets, and facilitate capital formation. As more and more first-time investors turn to the markets to help secure their futures, pay for homes, and send children to college, our investor protection mission is more compelling than ever. As our nation's securities exchanges mature into global for-profit competitors, there is even greater need for sound market regulation. And the common interest of all Americans in a growing economy that produces jobs, improves our standard of living, and protects the value of our savings means that all of the SEC's actions must be taken with an eye toward promoting the capital formation that is necessary to sustain economic growth.

▪ **SEC Military Site**: Offers warnings about scams that target members of the military, as well as general investor education and tips on how to check out a broker. *http://www.sec.gov/investor/military.shtml*

U.S. GENERAL SERVICES ADMINISTRATION OFFICE OF SMALL BUSINESS UTILIZATION (OSBU)

▪ *http://www.gsa.gov/portal/content/104628*

The OSBU advocates for small, small disadvantaged, veteran, service-disabled veteran-owned, HUBZone, and women business owners. The office provides increased access for small businesses to GSA's nationwide procurement opportunities. At OSBU, small businesses can take advantage of procurement networking sessions, marketing strategies and techniques workshops, electronic commerce/electronic data interchange training sessions, interagency networking, trade missions, roundtables, and procurement conferences, and social media tools to enhance their business.

U.S. SMALL BUSINESS ADMINISTRATION (SBA)

▪ *http://www.sba.gov*

The SBA helps members of the National Guard or Reserves (& their family) who own a small business, want to start a small business, or are an essential employee in a small business. SBA provides business planning and training programs and special financing to help start, grow or prepare their small business to overcome economic damage from Title 10 activations. Services and resources provided by the SBA include:

▪ **SBA's Office of Veterans Business Development (OVBD)**: coordinates and provides outreach, programs, and policy recommendations to SBA for veterans and members of Reserve components, & their families. *http://www.sba.gov/vets*

- **SBA District Offices:** coordinate access to 3500+local business assistance and financing partners who provide business counseling, planning, training, and financing options to help you start, grow, prepare for or recover from a call up. To locate your local district office, visit *http://www.sba.gov/about-offices-list/2*, or visit *http://www.sba.gov/direct*, and enter your zip code.

- **Small Business Development Centers (SBDC):** supported by the SBA and located in communities throughout the country. SBDCs provide management assistance to current and prospective small business owners and offer one-stop assistance to individuals and small businesses by providing a wide variety of information and guidance in central and easily accessible branch locations. *http://www.sba.gov/content/small-business-development-center-sbdcs-asbdc-us.org*

- **SCORE:** A non-profit organization that provides free mentoring services to entrepreneurs. Services are provided mainly by volunteers who have extensive knowledge and experience in operating businesses. You can link with a mentor through a local SCORE office. The website also provides numerous resources and tools to assist with starting a business. *http://www.score.org*

- **Veteran Business Development Officers (VBDOs):** Stationed at every SBA district office to guide you to local resources and program partners. *http://www.sba.gov/about-offices-content/1/2985/resources/47731*

- **Veteran Business Outreach Centers (VBOCs):** Designed to provide entrepreneurial development services such as business training, counseling and mentoring, and referrals for eligible veterans owning or considering starting a small business. The SBA has 16 organizations participating in this cooperative agreement and serving as VBOC. *http://www.sba.gov/content/veterans-business-outreach-centers*

- **Women's Business Center (WBCs):** Represent a national network of nearly 110 centers located at nonprofits across the country. Designed to assist women and men start and grow small businesses. *http://www.sba.gov/about-offices-content/1/2895*

- **SBA Micro Lenders:** Provides community mission-based lenders with capital to provide loans to borrowers up to $50K each, while providing required small business counseling and training. *http://www.sba.gov/content/microloan-program*

- ■ **Military Reservist Economic Injury Disaster Loans (MREIDL):** SBA direct loans for small businesses damaged by a Title 10 activation of the owner or essential employees. *http://www.sba.gov/about-offices-content/1/2985/resources/14807*

- ■ **Other SBA Loan and Surety Bond Guarantees:**

  - ■ **SBA Patriot Express Initiative:** Established by the SBA to assist members of the military community start a business or expand an existing business. It can be used for most business purposes, including start-up, expansion, equipment purchases, working capital, inventory or business-occupied real-estate purchases. *http://www.sba.gov/patriotexpress/sba_patriot_expressloan.html*

  - ■ **Surety Bonds:** An instrument that is signed by the Principal (or Contractor) and the Surety Company in order to protect the interests of the Obligee (the buyer, or party issuing the contract) in the event the Principal defaults on the contract. If the Principal defaults, the Surety Company steps in to ensure the contract is completed. *http://www.sba.gov/category/navigation-structure/loans-grants/bonds/surety-bonds*

  - ■ **Government Contracting Programs:** For women, for service-disabled veterans, for HUBZone firms, for 8(a) firms, & for small disadvantaged businesses. *http://www.sba.gov/about-offices-content/1/2986*

  - ■ The SBA also administers additional loan programs. *http://www.sba.gov/category/navigation-structure/loans-grants*

U.S. COPYRIGHT OFFICE

- ■ *http://www.copyright.gov/*

The U.S. Copyright Office promotes progress of the arts and protection for the works of authors. The site provides information about online registration options and other news about reengineering. It also offers informational circulars, application forms for copyright registration, links to the copyright law and to the homepages of other copyright-related organizations, a link to online copyright records cataloged since 1978, and much more.

U.S. WOMEN'S CHAMBER OF COMMERCE

- ■ *http://uswcc.org/*

The fundamental activity of the U.S. Women's Chambers of Commerce is to develop and implement policy on major issues affecting business.

Ten key issues/challenges the organization focusing on include education, workforce, energy and environment, infrastructure, legal reform, capital markets, health care, intellectual property, trade, economy & taxes. Also look into your local city chamber of commerce. You can locate policies, laws, resource, news, and information regarding a specific issue you may encounter in the set-up and/or operation of your business.

U.S. PATENT AND TRADEMARK OFFICE (USPTO)

http://www.uspto.gov/

The USPTO is the Federal agency for granting U.S. patents and registering trademarks. The USPTO furthers effective intellectual property (IP) protection for U.S. innovators and entrepreneurs worldwide by working with other agencies to secure strong IP provisions in free trade and other international agreements. It also provides training, education, and capacity building programs.

VOCATIONAL REHABILITATION (VR)

http://www.workworld.org/

Individuals with disabilities have access to federal and state funded VR services in communities nationwide. Agencies providing this service are administered on the state level and have branches located throughout each state. VR counselors at each branch offer services including career planning, job placement assistance, assistive and adaptive technology and financial assistance with school tuition. Branches also provide support and/or financial assistance to entrepreneurs planning to start a business. It is helpful to review your state VR organization's policy regarding self-employment to better understand the organization's role and parameters in assisting individuals with starting a business.

WORLD INSTITUTE ON DISABILITY (WID)

http://www.wid.org/programs/access-to-assets

The WID eliminates barriers to full social integration and increases employment, economic security and health care for persons with disabilities. WID creates innovative programs and tools; conducts research, public education, training and advocacy campaigns; and provides technical assistance.

WORK OPPORTUNITIES TAX CREDIT (WOTC)

■ *http://www.doleta.gov/business/Incentives/opptax*

The WOTC is a Federal tax credit incentive that Congress provides to private-sector businesses for hiring individuals from twelve target groups who have consistently faced significant barriers to employment. The main objective of this program is to enable the targeted employees to gradually move from economic dependency into self-sufficiency as they earn a steady income and become contributing taxpayers, while the participating employers are compensated by being able to reduce their federal income tax liability.

WORKWORLD: INDIVIDUAL TRAINING ACCOUNT (ITA) AT THE VIRGINIA COMMONWEALTH UNIVERSITY

■ *http://WorkWorld.org*

An ITA is an expenditure account established on behalf of a participant in a One-Stop Career Center. This site provides information on eligible training providers, the roles of customers/staff/board, a full glossary of terms, and a Disability Program Navigator (DPN).

Financing or Funding Resources

Resources and information cover a wide range of financial topics, including major business programs/initiatives for veteran/disability self-employers, technical assistance, tools, and training programs, financial literacy programs, and major personal/business finance websites.

ABILITIES FUND

■ *http://www.abilitiesfund.org/programs_and_services/lending.php*

The Abilities Fund is the first nationwide nonprofit community developer and financial institution focused exclusively on expanding entrepreneurial opportunities, including access to capital, for people with disabilities. The organization provides a unique combination of financial products, training, technical assistance services and advisory supports to individuals with disabilities. The Abilities Fund provides numerous business development tools as well as lending services.

ASSET DEVELOPMENT AND ACCUMULATION

■ **Free Volunteer Income Tax Assistance (VITA):** for low-income, people with disabilities, the elderly, and ESL. *http://www.vita-volunteers.org/index.htm*

■ **Earned Income Tax Credit (EITC):** Refundable tax credit on earned income (i.e., salary, tips and wages). *http://www.irs.gov/individuals/article/0,,id=96406,00.html*

■ **Consumer Advocacy and Protection:** Opt-out of solicitations and offers. *http://www.donotcall.gov/http://www.optoutprescreen.com,* 1(888) 567-8688

CREDIT COUNSELING AND DEBT MANAGEMENT

Consumer Credit Counseling Services (CCCS) near you, contact the following:

■ **Money Management International (MMI):** *http://www.moneymanagement.org*

■ **National Foundation for Credit Counseling (NFCC):** *http://www.nfcc.org*

CREDIT REPORTING AND CREDIT SCORING AGENCIES

Annual Credit Report: To obtain a free copy of your credit report (only, without the score): *http://www.AnnualCreditReport.com,* 1-877-322-8228

■ **Experian:** *http://www.Experian.com*

■ **Equifax:** *http://www.Equifax.com*

■ **FICO (Fair, Isaacs & Co.):** To obtain a copy of your credit score (fee-based): *http://www.myfico.com*

■ **TransUnion:** *http://www.Transunion.com*

FEDERAL GOVERNMENT AND NATIONAL FINANCIAL LITERACY RESOURCES

■ **360 Degrees of Financial Literacy:** For Military and Reserves, Parents & Children, Teens & Tweens, College Students, Couples, Retirees, etc. Provided by the American Institute of Certified Public Accountants. *http://www.360financialliteracy.org*

- **Credit Union National Association** Financial literacy resource for children, youth/young adults, families: *http://cuna.org/finlit/youth*

- **Financial Literacy & Education Commission** (clearinghouse of federal websites): *http://www.MyMoney.gov*, 1-888-MyMoney

FINANCIAL ORGANIZATIONS

- Compensation research tools to aid in salary negotiation: *http://www.salary.com* / *http://www.Payscale.com*

- **National Association of Professional Organizers (NAPO):** Locate a professional organizer near you who specializes in working with clients who have ADD. *http://www.NAPO.net*

IDENTITY AND CYBER-THEFT

- *http://www.identitytheft.info/federal.aspx*

Clearinghouse of federal resources on Identity and Cyber-Theft Protection and Prevention. Protect your Identity Week sponsored in part by the National Foundation for Credit Counseling, Inc. (NFCC) *http://www.protectyouridnow.org*

INDIVIDUAL DEVELOPMENT ACCOUNT (IDA)

- *http://www.cfed.org/*

An IDA is a savings account plan that is used to help establish cash savings to support and cover business expenses. To participate, individuals are required to establish a savings plan and to meet a savings requirement. The money deposited to this savings account must be earned income from wages rather than income set aside from public benefits payments. After at least six months of savings, the money deposited is matched at least 1:1 through the IDA program. That means, by the time you meet the required minimum $1000 in deposits, you will have at least $2000 in your account specifically to cover business expenses. Not all individuals qualify for an IDA—qualification depends on current income sources, benefits and savings. In addition, not all banks and credit unions offer IDAs. If an institution in your locale offers IDAs, a representative there can assist you in evaluating your current circumstances as they relate to opening an IDA.

ADDITIONAL RESOURCES

▓ **BankRate:** Financial calculator for home mortgage/re-financing, vehicle, CDs and investments, credit cards, college loans, bank rates, etc. *http://www.BankRate.com.*

▓ **Credit Card Rate Comparison Sites:**

    ▓ *http://www.Credit.com*

    ▓ *http://www.CardTrak.com*

    ▓ *http://www.CardWeb.com*

▓ **The Consumer Financial Emergency Survival Kit:** *http://www.bos/ frb.org/consumer/survival-guide/index.htm*

Job Accommodation

Technical assistance, consultancy, and resources provided by national/ local career centers or shared within the online community.

ONE-STOP CAREER CENTERS

▓ *http://www.careeronestop.org*

One-Stop Career Centers ("One-Stops") are located in communities throughout the country and were created by a federal mandate in order to centralize information and services on career services and workforce development. One-Stops offer numerous free services including career counseling, job referrals and computer training classes. Most DVOP Specialists are located at One-Stops. In addition, Disability Program Navigators are located at all One-Stops and provide additional support services to individuals with disabilities. One-Stops are also home to Local Veterans' Employment Representatives (LVERs) who are responsible for assisting and advocating for Veterans who access services at the One-Stop.

JOB ACCOMMODATION NETWORK (JAN)

▓ *http://www.jan.wvu.edu*

JAN provides free, expert, and confidential guidance on workplace accommodations and disability employment issues. JAN's trusted consultants offer one-on-one guidance on workplace accommodations, the Americans with Disabilities Act (ADA), related legislation, and self-employment and entrepreneurship options for people with disabilities. Assistance is available both over the phone and online.

U.S. DEPARTMENT OF LABOR OFFICE OF DISABILITY EMPLOYMENT POLICY

■ *http://www.dol.gov/odep*

Provides information on entrepreneurship, customized employment-links to JAN, and other employer resources.

WORKSUPPORT.COM

■ *http://www.worksupport.com*

Information on work place supports training and technical assistance in rehabilitation for individuals with disabilities.

Legal Assistance for Start-up Companies

ALLLAW

■ *http://www.alllaw.com*

AllLaw is the Internet's premier Law portal. This site provides a broad range of legal topics, advice, current trends, and a comprehensive list of attorneys throughout the U.S. and Canada.

CORNELL UNIVERSITY LAW SCHOOL

■ *http://www.lawschool.cornell.edu*

The Cornell University Law School website introduces the people who are involved in maintaining Cornell's status as a premier legal institution. Meet the faculty and students, browse legal journals, and read about the successful graduates who continue their commitment to the Law School.

FINDLAW

■ *http://www.findlaw.com*

FindLaw provides legal information, lawyer profiles, and a community to assist in making the best legal decisions. They also offer interactive videos and Law blogs.

HG LEGAL DIRECTORIES
■ *http://www.hg.org*

HG Legal Directories was one of the very first online law and government sites. It was founded in January of 1995 by Lex Mundi, a large network of independent law firms. The HG Legal Directories objective is to make law, government and related professional information easily accessible to the legal profession, businesses and consumers.

KUESTERLAW
■ *http://www.kuesterlaw.com*

KuesterLaw is known as the technology resource. This site is intended to be the most comprehensive resource on the Internet for technology law information, especially including patent, copyright, and trademark law.

NOLO
■ *http://www.nolo.com*

Nolo is passionate about making the law accessible to everyone. Their high-quality books, software, legal forms, and online lawyer directory have helped millions of people find answers to their everyday legal and business questions.

SMARTPROS
■ *http://www.smartpros.com*

SmartPros provides continuing professional education and corporate training. Their topics include accounting and finance, financial services, engineering, legal and ethics, and information technology.

Not-For Profits

ASSOCIATION OF UNIVERSITY CENTERS ON DISABILITIES (AUCD)
■ *http://www.aucd.org/template/page.cfm?id=667*

The association encompasses University Centers for Excellence in Developmental Disabilities (UCEDDs), which work with people with disabilities, members of their families, state and local government agencies, and community providers in projects that provide training, technical assistance, service, research, and information sharing, with a focus on

CHAPTER 5

building the capacity of communities to sustain all their citizens. Currently, there are 67 UCEDDs across the country.

BURTON BLATT INSTITUTE AT SYRACUSE UNIVERSITY (BBI)

■ *http://bbi.syr.edu*

The BBI at Syracuse University works on advancing the civic, economic, and social participation of people with disabilities. The BBI website contains articles on disability, diversity, reasonable accommodations, employment, and entrepreneurship.

INSTITUTE FOR VETERANS AND MILITARY FAMILIES AT SYRACUSE UNIVERSITY (IVMF)

■ *http://vets.syr.edu*

The first academic center in higher education focused on research, education, and employment for veterans and military families. The IVMF offers multiple education programs in veteran entrepreneurship.

NATIONAL COALITION FOR HOMELESS VETERANS (NCHV)

■ *http://www.nchv.org*

NCHV provides resources and technical assistance for nation-wide community-based service providers and local, state and federal agencies that provide emergency and supportive housing, food, health services, job training and placement assistance, legal aid and case management support for homeless veterans each year. NCHV also provides information, counseling, medical assistance for homeless veterans, as well as technical assistance for veteran employment. Find a local homeless veteran program coordinator, please visit: *http://www.nchv.org/veterans.cfm*.

Other Resources

ALLBUSINESS

■ *http://www.allbusiness.com*

AllBusiness is the world's largest online resource for small businesses, providing essential tools and resources to start, grow, and manage a business. The site includes helpful advice in topics such as sales and marketing, human resources and technology. There is also a large business library, weekly special reports on important trends, and videos and podcasts.

AMERICA'S HEROES AT WORK

http://www.americasheroesatwork.gov

America's Heroes at Work is a DOL project that addresses the employment challenges of returning Service Members and Veterans living with Traumatic Brain Injury (TBI) and/or Post-Traumatic Stress Disorder (PTSD). Designed for employers and the workforce development system, this website is your link to information and tools to help returning Service Members and Veterans living with TBI and/or PTSD succeed in the workplace—particularly Service Members returning from Iraq and Afghanistan.

BATTLEMIND

Training that helps military personnel make the transition from skills needed for survival on the battlefield to those that are needed for success in the home, community and workplace.

Training I
Transitioning from Combat to Home
http://www.behavioralhealth.army.mil/battlemind/WRAIR_Battle mind_Training_I_Brochure_Final.pdf

Training II
Continuing the Transition Home
http://www.behavioralhealth.army.mil/battlemind/Battlemind TrainingII.pdf

GAEBLER VENTURES

http://www.gaeblervc.com/Entrepreneurs.htm

Gaebler Ventures is a business incubator and holding company that develops and nurtures companies. With an emphasis on seed-stage and early-stage investments, the Chicago-based partnership has invested in companies since 1999 and has established numerous innovative and market-leading enterprises.

INVISIBLE WOUNDS OF WAR PSYCHOLOGICAL AND COGNITIVE INJURIES, THEIR CONSEQUENCES, AND SERVICES TO ASSIST RECOVERY

http://www.rand.org/pubs/monographs/MG720.html

The RAND conducted a comprehensive study of the post-deployment health-related needs associated with these three conditions among OEF/

OIF veterans, the health care system in place to meet those needs, gaps in the care system, and the costs associated with these conditions and with providing quality health care to all those in need.

NATIONAL VETERANS TECHNICAL ASSISTANCE CENTER (NVTAC)

http://bbi.syr.edu/nvtac

NVTAC provides technical assistance to current grantees and potential applicants as well as information to the public; gathers grantee best practices; conducts employment-related research on homeless Veterans; conducts regional grantee training sessions and conferences; and coordinates efforts with various local, state and federal social service providers.

SAMHSA MILITARY FAMILIES

http://www.samhsa.gov/MilitaryFamilies

Supporting America's service men and women—Active Duty, National Guard, Reserve, and Veteran—together with their families and communities by leading efforts to ensure that needed behavioral health services are accessible and that outcomes are positive.

THE DISABLED VETERANS NATIONAL FOUNDATION

http://www.fedshirevets.gov/.

The disable Veterans National Foundation exists to change the lives of men and women who came home wounded or sick after defending our safety and our freedom.

THE HUD-VETERANS AFFAIRS SUPPORTIVE HOUSING (HUD-VASH)

http://www.va.gov/homeless/hud-vash.asp

The HUD-VASH program combines Housing Choice Voucher (HCV) rental assistance for homeless veterans with case management and clinical services provided by the VA. VA provides these services for participating veterans at VA medical centers (VAMCs) and community-based outreach clinics.

THE VETERANS CRISIS LINE

http://veteranscrisisline.net

The Veterans Crisis Line connects veterans in crisis and their families and friends with qualified, caring VA responders through a confidential, toll-free hotline, online chat, or text. Veterans and their loved ones can call 1-800-273-8255 and Press 1, chat online, or send a text message to 838255 to receive confidential support 24 hours a day, 7 days a week, and 365 days a year.

U.S. ARMY MEDICAL DEPARTMENT, RESILIENCE TRAINING, ARMY BEHAVIORAL HEALTH

http://www.army.mil/article/25494/army-developing-master-resiliency-training

The Army has been working with the University of Pennsylvania to develop master resiliency training that will soon be taught to Soldiers, family members and Army civilians. The resiliency training is part of Comprehensive Soldier Fitness, which focuses on the five dimensions of strength: emotional, social, spiritual, family and physical.

VETERANS' MENTAL HEALTH CARE EMPHASIZES RECOVERY AND RETURN TO FULL AND MEANINGFUL LIVES

http://www.apa.org/news/press/releases/2011/11/recovery-return.aspx

Six questions for VA's chief consultant of Mental Health Services how the science of psychology is helping service members adjust to life at home after the trauma of war.

Resources for Veteran Employment or Self-Employment

CESSI ACCESSIBLE SOLUTIONS

http://www.cessi.net/contracts/pm/ssa_pmro.html

Cessi offers information on the Ticket to Work Program Manager for Recruitment and Outreach (PMRO). The Ticket Program provides disability beneficiaries with choices for receiving employment services and increases provider incentive to serve these individuals. Under the Ticket Program, the Agency is directed to provide disability beneficiaries with a Ticket they may use to obtain VR services, employment services, and/ or other support services from an EN of their choice and to establish agreements with ENs to provide such services.

CUSTOMIZED EMPLOYMENT (CE)

http://www.dol.gov/odep/alliances/ce.htm

CE includes the process of 'discovery' that can help Veterans identify their inherent strengths, gifts, skills and support needs and customize jobs that make sense for both the job-seeker and employer.

DIVERSITY INC.

■ *http://diversityinc.com*

Diversity, Inc. is a consultancy business, providing information and education on the business benefits of diversity, including employees with disabilities. The company publishes two websites: ***www.Diversity-Inc.com*** and ***www.DiversityIncBestPractices.com***, as well as Diversity, Inc. Magazine, published five times a year. It also organizes and produces events addressing diversity issues at the workplace.

ENTREPRENEURSHIP BOOTCAMP FOR VETERANS' FAMILIES (EBV-F)

■ *http://whitman.syr.edu/ebv/programs/families/*

The EBV-F is an education and training program founded at SU's Whitman School. The program is designed to leverage the flexibility inherent in small business ownership to provide a vocational and economic path forward for military family members who are now caregivers to a wounded warrior, or for surviving spouses of a military member who gave his or her life in service to our country. The EBV-F integrates training in small business management, with caregiver and family issues, positioning the family member to launch and grow a small business in a way that is complementary or enhancing to other family responsibilities. Modeled after the existing EBV program, the EBV-F is offered without any cost to accepted applicants. The EBV-F is currently offered at Syracuse University and Florida State University. Visit the EBV-F website for more information and to apply.

ENTREPRENEURSHIP BOOTCAMP FOR VETERANS WITH DISABILITIES (EBV)

■ *http://whitman.syr.edu/ebv/*

The EBV was developed as an intensive training program positioned to offer cutting-edge, experiential training in entrepreneurship and small business management to post-9/11 veterans disabled as a result of service to our country. The program represents a 14-month 'intervention' and includes online coursework, a nine-day residency at a host EBV university and post-residency mentorship for a period of at least 12 months. The program was founded at SU's Whitman School and is offered entirely free to qualified, accepted veterans through a national consortium of seven world-class business and hospitality schools across the country: Syracuse University, Florida State University, the University of California, Los Angeles, Texas A&M University, Purdue University, the University of Connecticut, Louisiana State University and Cornell University. Visit the EBV website for more information and to apply.

ENTREPRENEURSHIP FOR VETERANS WITH DISABILITIES: LESSONS LEARNED FROM THE FIELD NATIONAL TECHNICAL ASSISTANCE AND RESOURCE CENTER

https://www.dol.gov/odep/documents/NTAR_Issue_Brief_1_Veterans.pdf

This brief examines entrepreneurship as a viable option for veterans with disabilities, particularly those returning from the present-day conflicts in the Middle East.

FEDS HIRE VETS

http://www.fedshirevets.gov/

Feds Hire Vets is your single site for Federal employment information for Veterans, transitioning military service members, their families, and Federal hiring officials.

START-UP NY/INCLUSIVE ENTREPRENEURSHIP

http://bbi.syr.edu/startupny/

'Start-UP NY'/Inclusive Entrepreneurship' demonstrated out-comes in helping Veterans and non-Veterans with disabilities develop their own small businesses.

SUPPORTED EMPLOYMENT

http://store.samhsa.gov/product/Supported-Employment-Evidence-Based-Practices-EBP-KIT/SMA08-4365

Supported Employment (SE) is an evidence based practice that can improve employment outcomes for Veterans—especially those with mental health issues served through Vocational Rehabilitation (VR) programs.

VETERANS' EMPLOYMENT & TRAINING SERVICE (VETS)

http://www.dol.gov/vets/

Veterans' Employment & Training Service (VETS) is a clearinghouse website for the range of employment services offered through the Department of Labor/VETS.

NATIONAL VETERAN-OWNED BUSINESS ASSOCIATION (NAVOBA)

http://www.navoba.com

NaVOBA's mission is simple: to create opportunities for all of America's veteran-owned businesses.

OPERATION ENDURE & GROW

■ *http://www.whitman.syr.edu/endureandgrow/*

Operation Endure & Grow is an online training experience focused on the fundamentals of launching and/or growing a small business. The eight-week training program is open to National Guard and Reserve service members and their immediate family members. The program runs every eight weeks with 50-seat per term course offerings alternating between a start-up-focused curriculum and a growth/sustain-orientated curriculum. The cost to participants is minimal; they are responsible for a $75.00 registration fee per term. Visit the Operation Endure & Grow website for more information and to apply.

SELF EMPLOYMENT TECHNICAL ASSISTANCE AND TRAINING CENTER (START-UP USA)

■ *http://www.start-up-usa.biz/*

START-UP USA provides technical assistance and disseminates resources nationally to individuals interested in pursuing self-employment. This includes a series of live webinar training sessions addressing issues in self-employment for veterans with disabilities, financing a business, benefits planning, and family support for the self-employment.

VETERAN WOMEN IGNITING THE SPIRIT OF ENTREPRENEURSHIP (V-WISE)

■ *http://whitman.syr.edu/vwise/*

V-WISE is a premier training program in entrepreneurship and small business management. The program is open to all women veterans, active duty females or female partners/spouses of active duty or veteran military personnel who are interested in learning about entrepreneurship and starting, running or growing a business. Participants may be from any branch of the military and across any era of service. The training consists of three phases: online, conference and mentorship. The cost to participants is minimal; they are responsible for a $75.00 registration fee and their transportation to and from the conference. All other expenses are covered, i.e. hotel, books and food. Visit the V-WISE website for more information and to apply.

Social Security Administration Disability Benefit

PASS ONLINE AT CORNELL UNIVERSITY

http://www.passonline.org

The Plan for Achieving Self Support (PASS) is an SSI work incentive that teaches users how to use their own income or assets to help them reach their work goals. This website provides basic information about a PASS, and a PASS application form.

PASSPLAN AT THE UNIVERSITY OF MONTANA RURAL INSTITUTE

http://www.passplan.org

Plan for Achieving Self Support (PASS) allows a person with a disability to set aside otherwise countable income and/or resources for a specific period of time in order to achieve a work goal. Any person who receives SSI benefits, or who might qualify for SSI, or any person receives who SSDI (or a similar benefit) and could qualify for SSI, may be able to have a PASS. There is no limit to the number of successful PASS plans a person may use in a lifetime.

THE RED BOOK – A GUIDE TO WORK INCENTIVES

http://www.socialsecurity.gov/redbook

The Red Book Publication is the SSA's guide for employment-related work incentives. The Red Book serves as a general reference source about the employment-related provisions of Social Security Disability Insurance and the Supplemental Security Income Programs for educators, advocates, rehabilitation professionals, and counselors who serve people with disabilities.

WORK INCENTIVES PLANNING AND ASSISTANCE (WIPA)

http://www.socialsecurity.gov/work/wipafactsheet.html

The WIPA projects across the U.S. and the U.S. territories work with SSA beneficiaries with disabilities on job placement, benefits planning, and career development.

CHAPTER 5

VA Disability Benefit

BLINDED VETERANS ASSOCIATION (BVA)

http://www.bva.org/index.html

The BVA is an organization of blinded veterans helping blinded veterans through service programs, regional groups, resources, and advocacy before the legislative and executive branches of government. All legally blinded veterans are also eligible for BVA's assistance whether they become blind during or after active duty military service.

CONCURRENT RETIREMENT AND DISABILITY PAY (CRDP)

http://www.military.com/benefits/content/military-pay/concurrent-retirement-and-disability-pay-crdp-overview.html

The Concurrent Receipt means to receive both military retirement benefits and VA disability compensation.

DEPARTMENT OF DEFENSE PERSONNEL AND READINESS

http://prhome.defense.gov/

The DoD Personnel and Readiness develop policies and plans, conduct analyses, provide advice, make recommendations, and issue guidance on DoD plans and programs.

DISABLED AMERICAN VETERANS (DAV)

http://www.dav.org/

The DAV is a 1.2 million-member non-profit charity dedicated to building better lives for America's disabled veterans and their families. This site provides information on benefits assistance programs, as well as a comprehensive list of volunteer services programs.

FEDERAL BENEFITS FOR VETERANS, DEPENDENTS, AND SURVIVORS

http://www.va.gov/opa/publications/benefits_book.asp.

MILITARY COMPENSATION

http://militarypay.defense.gov/Retirement/concurrent_dod_va.html

The Military Pay and Benefits Website is sponsored by the Office of the Under Secretary of Defense for Personnel and Readiness. The major elements of compensation (pay, retirement, and benefits) are discussed.

PARALYZED VETERANS OF AMERICA (PVA)

▓ *http://www.pva.org/site/PageServer?pagename=homepage*

PVA provides veterans with secure benefits that have been denied. They also offer vocational rehabilitation counselors to help veterans get back to work.

U.S. DEPARTMENT OF LABOR ONE-STOPS MAP

▓ *http://www.doleta.gov/usworkforce/onestop/onestopmap.cfm*

Interactive map allows users to click on their individual state to find unemployment insurance filing information.

U.S. DEPARTMENT OF VETERANS AFFAIRS (VA)

▓ *http://www.va.gov/*

The State VA offices provide information on VA disability benefits and State VA benefits planning.

▓ **Veterans Affairs Forms**
Provides information on how and where to submit your VA forms. *http://www.va.gov/vaforms/*

State Resources

STATE VETERANS' BENEFITS DIRECTORY

▓ *http://www.military.com/benefits/veteran-benefits/state-veterans-benefits-directory*

Each state manages its own veterans' benefit programs. Site provides a list of links to websites for individual states that offer these benefits.

STATE VOCATIONAL REHABILITATION AGENCIES

▓ *http://www.workworld.org/wwwebhelp/state_vocational_rehabilitation_vr_agencies.htm*

▓ ALABAMA

Alabama Department of Revenue:
http://www.revenue.alabama.gov/

SBA Office:
http://www.sba.gov/vets

Alabama Small Business Development Consortium:
http://www.asbdc.org/

Office of Small Business Advocacy:
http://www.ado.alabama.gov/con
tent/ourservices/small_business/
smallbusiness.aspx

Alabama Department of Economic and Community Affairs:
http://www.adeca.state.al.us/default.
aspx

USDA Rural Development of Alabama:
http://www.rurdev.usda.gov/al/

Alabama Department of Industrial Relations:
http://dir.alabama.gov/ralbusiness/
default.aspx

Alabama Business Resource Center:
http://www.al.com/business/

Alabama Small Business Resource Development Center:
http://www.montgomerychamber.
com/Page.aspx?pid=465

Small Business Development Center at UA:
http://cba.ua.edu/sbdc/

Alabama Chamber of Commerce:
http://www.alabamachambers.org

Secretary of State:
http://www.sos.state.al.us

Central Alabama Women's Business Center:
http://www.cawbc.org

Women's Business Center of North Alabama:
http://www.wbcna.org

Women's Business Center of Southern Alabama:
http://www.womenbiz.biz/WBC-
SouthernAlabama.html

▦ ALASKA

State of Alaska Business:
http://alaska.gov/businessHome.html

Alaska SBDC:
http://www.aksbdc.org

Alaska SourceLink:
http://www.aksourcelink.com

Economic Development and Commerce:
http://www.commerce.state.ak.us

Small Business Assistance Center:
http://www.commerce.state.ak.us/ded/
dev/smallbus/home.cfm

Alaska Industrial Development and Export Authority:
http://www.aidea.org

Training and Employment Program:
http://labor.alaska.gov/bp/programs.
htm

Alaska Veterans Business Alliance:
http://www.akvba.org

Chamber of Commerce:
http://www.alaskachamber.com

Women's Business Solutions:
http://www.ywcaak.org/finances.htm

▦ ARIZONA

Department of Veterans' Services:
http://www.azdvs.gov/VetBiz/Business
_Resources.aspx

Arizona Business Resource List:
http://az.gov/business.html

Arizona Entrepreneurs Business Resources:
http://www.azbusinessresource.com/

Arizona Small Business Association:
http://www.asba.com

Arizona Business Association:
http://www.abasafety.com

Chamber of Commerce:
http://www.azchamber.com

Secretary of State:
http://www.azsos.gov

Microbusiness Advancement Center of Southern Arizona:
http://www.mac-sa.org

ARKANSAS

Arkansas Small Business and Technology Development Center:
http://asbtdc.org/

Arkansas Department of Veterans Affairs:
http://www.veterans.arkansas.gov/sba.html

Arkansas Veteran:
http://arkansasveteran.com/business

University of Arkansas SBTDC:
http://sbtdc.uark.edu/

University of Arkansas Community and Economic Development:
http://arcommunities.com/

Arkansas Veteran Resources:
http://arkansasveteran.com/about/partnerships/asbtdc

ASBTDC Veteran Loans:
http://asbdc.ualr.edu/veterans/

Chamber of Commerce:
www.arkansasstatechamber.com

Secretary of State:
www.sos.arkansas.gov

Winrock International:
http://www.winrock.org

CALIFORNIA

Secretary of State:
http://www.sos.ca.gov

Chamber of Commerce:
http://www.calchamber.com

California SBDC:
http://www.californiasbdc.org

Small Business California:
http://www.smallbusinesscalifornia.org

California Tax Service Center:
http://www.taxes.ca.gov/Small_Business_Assistance_Center/index.shtml

Economic Workforce and Development:
http://www.cccewd.net

Veterans Business Outreach Center:
http://www.vboc-ca.org

California Disabled Veterans Business Alliance:
http://www.cadvbe.org

Asian Pacific Islander Small Business Program WBC:
http://www.apisbp.org/index.html

Coachella Valley Women's Business Center (CVWBC):
http://www.cvwbc.org/

Inland Empire Women's Business Center:
http://www.iewbc.org

Institute for Women Entrepreneurs:
http://www.ociwe.org

Mendocino Women's Business Center:
http://www.westcompany.org/wbc.php

PACE Women's Business Center:
http://www.pacelabdc.org/Home_Page.php

Renaissance Entrepreneurship Center:
http://www.rencenter.org/

Women Business Partners Program – San Luis Obispo:
http://www.mcscorp.org/

Women's Economic Ventures:
http://www.wevonline.org/

Women's Initiative for Self Employment:
http://www.womensinitiative.org/index.htm

Valley Economic Development Center:
http://www.vedc.org/

■ COLORADO

Colorado Small Business Development Center Network:
http://www.coloradosbdc.org/

North Colorado Entrepreneurs; Innovative Business Incubators:
http://rmi2.org/

The Business Incubator Center:
http://www.gjincubator.org/

Denver SBDC:
http://www.smallbusinessdenver.com

Office of Economic Development & International Trade:
http://www.colorado.gov/cs/Satellite/OEDIT/OEDIT/1162927366334

Chamber of Commerce:
http://www.cochamber.com

Doing Business in Denver:
http://www.denvergov.org/DoingBusinessinDenver/tabid/435548/Default.aspx

Secretary of State Business Licensing Center:
http://www.sos.state.co.us/pubs/BusinessAndLicensing/main.html

Northern Colorado Business Start-Up:
http://libguidescolostate.edu/content php?pid=44495&sid=1883906

Secretary of State:
http://www.sos.state.co.us

Mi Casa Resource Center for Women Inc.:
http://www.micasadenver.org

■ CONNECTICUT

Connecticut Small Business Development Center:
http://www.ctsbdc.org/

The Connecticut Business & Industry Association:
http://www.cbia.com/home.php

Community Economic Development Fund:
http://www.cedf.com/

Connecticut Economic Resource Center:
http://www.cerc.com/

Doing Business in CT:
http://www.ct.gov/ctportal/taxono
my/taxonomy.asp?DLN=27187&
ctportalNav=%7C27187%7C

Women's Business Development Center:
http://www.ctwbdc.org

University of Hartford Entrepreneurial Center:
http://www.hartford.edu/cpd/ec/

Connecticut Center for Advanced Technology:
http://www.ccat.us

Connecticut Innovations:
http://www.ctinnovations.com

Department of Veterans Affairs:
http://www.ct.gov/ctva/site/default.asp

CT Business & Industry:
http://www.cbia.com

Connecticut Development Authority:
http://www.ctcda.com

Secretary of State:
http://www.ct.gov/sots

Stamford/Southwest Women's Business Center:
http://www.ctwbdc.org

Naugatuck Valley Women's Business Center:
http://www.ctwbdc.org

▓ DELAWARE

Delaware SBTDC:
http://www.dsbtdc.org

Delaware PTAC:
http://www.delawarecontracts.com

Economic Development Office:
http://www.dedo.delaware.gov

Secretary of State:
http://http://sos.delaware.gov/

Chamber of Commerce:
http://www.dscc.com

Center for Women's Entrepreneurship:
http://www.ywca.org/sitepp.asp?c=
gjIQI4PKKoG&b=1721117

▓ DISTRICT OF COLUMBIA

DC Women's Business Center:
http://www.dcwbc.org

▓ FLORIDA

Florida Small Business:
http://www.floridatrend.com/small_
biz.asp

Small Business Development Center at the University of Florida:
http://www.sbdctampabay.com/

Florida Business Incubation Association:
http://www.fbiaonline.org/

Florida Small Business Development Center Network:
http://floridasbdc.org/intro.html

Florida Department of Veterans Affairs:
http://www.floridavets.org

Enterprise Florida:
http://www.eflorida.com

CHAPTER 5

Florida Small Business:
http://www.floridasmallbusiness.com

Workforce Florida:
http://www.workforceflorida.com

Department of State:
http://www.dos.state.fl.us

Chamber of Commerce:
http://www.flchamber.com

Florida Women's Business Center:
http://www.flwbc.org

Jacksonville Women's Business Center:
http://www.myjaxchamber.com

Women's Business Center:
http://www.wbc.fit.edu

GEORGIA

Georgia Chamber of Commerce:
http://www.gachamber.com/

Small Business Development Center (West Georgia University):
http://www.westga.edu/sbdc/

Georgia Small Business Development Center:
http://www.georgiasbdc.org

Starting a Business in Georgia:
http://www.georgia.org/Business InGeorgia/SmallBusiness/Business Resources/Pages/default.aspx

Georgia Business Resource Alliance:
http://www.gbra.com

Secretary of State:
http://www.sos.ga.gov/Corporations/

Women's Economic Development Agency Inc.:
http://www.weda-atlanta.org

The Edge Connection Inc.:
http://www.theedgeconnection.com

HAWAII

Chamber of Commerce:
http://www.cochawaii.com

Hawaii SBDC:
http://www.hisbdc.com

Small Business Innovation Research Program:
http://www.htdc.org/hawaii-sbir.html

Secretary of State:
http://hawaii.gov/ltgov/

Department of Business and Economic Development:
http://hawaii.gov/dbedt

Economic Development Board:
http://www.hiedb.org/

Enterprise Oahu:
http://www.enterprisehonolulu.com/

High Technology Development Center:
http://www.htdc.org

IDAHO

Idaho Small Business Solutions:
http://www.idahobizhelp.org

Idaho SBDC:
http://www.idahosbdc.org

Department of Commerce:
http://commerce.idaho.gov/

CHAPTER 5

Idaho Association of Commerce and Industry:
http://www.iaci.org/

Idaho Secretary of State:
http://www.sos.idaho.gov

ILLINOIS

Illinois Chamber of Commerce:
http://www.ilchamber.org

Secretary of State:
http://www.cyberdriveillinois.com

Department of Commerce:
http://www.commerce.state.il.us/dceo/

Illinois Small Business Development Center:
http://siusbdc.com/

University of Illinois College Small Business Development Center:
http://www.uic.edu/cba/cub/

Research Park Innovation Center:
http://researchpark.illinois.edu/

Women's Business Development Center:
http://www.wbdc.org

INDIANA

Indiana Chamber of Commerce:
http://www.indianachamber.com

Secretary of State:
http://www.in.gov/sos

Indiana SBDC:
http://www.isbdc.org

Purdue Technical Assistance Program:
http://www.tap.purdue.edu/

Venture Club of Indiana:
http://www.ventureclub.org/

Indiana Economic Development Association:
http://ieda.org/wp/

Indiana Finance Authority:
http://www.in.gov/ifa/

Cambridge Capital Management Corp.:
http://www.cambridgecapital mgmt.com/

Indiana University Business Resource Center:
http://www.ibrc.indiana.edu/

Women's Enterprise:
http://www.womensenterprise.org

Central Indiana Women's Business Center:
http://www.businessownership.org

IOWA

Iowa Economic Development Authority:
http://www.iowaeconomicdevelop ment.com/

New Ventures Inc:
http://www.newventuresinc.com/

Iowa Business & Development:
http://regassist.iowa.gov/

Iowa SBDC:
http://www.iowasbdc.org/

University of Northern Iowa Regional Business Center:
http://www.uni.edu/rbc

Iowa Center for Enterprise:
http://enterprise.uiowa.edu/

CHAPTER 5

Iowa Department of Veterans Affairs:
https://va.iowa.gov/

Secretary of State:
http://sos.iowa.gov/

Chamber of Commerce:
http://www.iowachamber.net

Iowa Women's Enterprise Center:
http://www.isediowa.org

KANSAS

Network Kansas:
http://www.networkkansas.com/

Kansas SBDC:
http://ksbdc.kansas.gov/Pages/default.aspx

Kansas Secretary of State:
http://www.kssos.org

Kansas Chamber of Commerce:
http://www.kansaschamber.org

KC SourceLink:
http://www.kcsourcelink.com

Kansas Business Center:
http://www.kansas.gov/businesscenter/starting/

Kansas Women's Business Center:
http://www.kansaswbc.com/

KENTUCKY

Community Ventures Corp.:
http://www.cvcky.org

LOUISIANA

Louisiana Economic Development:
http://www.louisianaeconomicdevelopment.com/

Louisiana Small Business Development Center:
https://www.lsbdc.org/

Southeastern Louisiana University Small Business Development Center:
http://www.selu.edu/admin/sbdc/

Louisiana Government Business:
http://www.louisiana.gov/wps/wcm/connect/Louisiana.gov/Business+in+Louisiana/

Louisiana Workforce Commission:
http://www.ldol.state.la.us/homepage.asp

Louisiana Veterans Business Outreach Center:
http://www.lvboc.net/home.html

Louisiana Department of Veterans Affairs:
http://www.vetaffairs.la.gov/

LSU Business School:
http://business.lsu.edu/

Chamber of Commerce:
http://www.cenlachamber.org

Secretary of State:
http://www.sos.la.gov

Enterprise Consortium of the Gulf Coast:
http://www.ecgcwbc.com

Women's Business Resource Center:
http://www.urbanleague neworleans.org/

MAINE

Maine SBDC:
http://www.mainesbdc.org

Small Business Assistance:
http://www.mainebusinessworks.
org

Maine Office of Business Development:
http://www.maine.gov/decd/

USM Center for Business and Economic Research:
http://www.usm.maine.edu/mcber/

Maine Technology Institute:
http://www.mainetechnology.org

Finance Authority of Maine:
http://www.famemaine.com

Chamber of Commerce:
http://www.mainechamber.org

Secretary of State:
http://www.maine.gov/sos

Southern Maine Women's Business Center at Coastal Enterprises Inc.:
http://www.wbcmaine.org

Rim Counties Women's Business Center at Coastal Enterprise Inc.:
http://www.wbcmaine.org

MARYLAND

SBDC Maryland:
http://www.mdsbdc.umd.edu/

Checklist for New Businesses Maryland:
http://www.dat.state.md.us/sdatweb/
checklist.html

Secretary of State:
http://www.sos.state.md.us/

List of Maryland Venture Capital Firms:
http://www.gaebler.com/Maryland-
venture-capital-firms.htm

Small Business Reserve Program:
https://www.smallbusinessreserve.
maryland.gov/index.cfm

Maryland Department of Business & Economic Development:
http://www.choosemaryland.org/
businessresources/pages/default.aspx

Maryland Department of Veterans Affairs:
http://www.mdva.state.md.us/

Secretary of State:
http://www.sos.state.md.us

Chamber of Commerce:
http://www.mdchamber.org

Women Entrepreneurs of Baltimore Inc.:
http://www.webinc.org

MASSACHUSETTS

Mass. Government Business Resources:
http://www.mass.gov/portal/business/

Massachusetts SBDC:
http://www.msbdc.org

Secretary of State:
http://www.mass.gov/sec

Massachusetts Growth Capital Corporation:
http://www.mcdfc.com/

Massachusetts Technology Collaborative:
http://www.masstech.org

Associated Industries of Massachusetts:
http://www.aimnet.org

Massachusetts Association of
Business Incubators:
http://www.massincubators.org

UMass Donahue Institute:
http://www.donahue.umassp.edu

Mass Capital Resource Company:
http://www.masscapital.com

Massachusetts; It's All Here:
http://www.massitsallhere.com

Directory of Local Chambers
of Commerce:
http://www.2chambers.com/
massachu2.htm

Center for Women & Enterprise:
http://www.cweonline.org

■ MICHIGAN

Michigan Economic Development
Corporation:
http://www.michiganadvantage.org/
Entrepreneurs-and-Innovators/

Michigan Small Business &
Technology Development Center:
http://misbtdc.org/

Michigan Government Business
& Economic Growth:
http://www.michigan.gov/
som/0,4669,7-192-29943---,00.html

Small Business Association of
Michigan:
http://www.sbam.org

Pure Michigan Veterans:
http://www.mitalent.org/Veterans/

VFW Michigan:
http://www.vfwmi.org/veteranjobs.
htm

Michigan Business One-Stop:
http://www.michigan.gov/business

Michigan State University
Business Connect:
http://www.businessconnect.msu.
edu/

Michigan Chamber of Commerce:
http://www.michamber.com/

Secretary of State:
http://www.michigan.gov/sos

Michigan Women's Marketplace:
http://www.miwomen.com

Grand Rapids Opportunities for
Women (GROW):
http://www.growbusiness.org

■ MINNESOTA

Minnesota Chamber of
Commerce:
http://www.mnchamber.com

Secretary of State:
http://www.sos.state.mn.us

Twin Cities Business:
http://www.tcbmag.com

New Business Minnesota:
http://www.newbizminn.com/

Sustainable Business Resource
Center:
http://www.sbrcmn.com

Women's Business Development
Center:
http://www.wbdc.org

Minnesota SBDC:
http://www.mnsbdc.com

Center for Rural Entrepreneurial Studies:
http://www.umccres.org

WomenVenture:
http://www.womenventure.org

Women's Business Center:
http://www.entrepreneurfund.org/

■ MISSISSIPPI

Mississippi SBDC:
http://www.mssbdc.org

Secretary of State:
http://www.sos.ms.gov

Chamber of Commerce:
http://www.msmec.com

Mississippi Development Authority:
http://www.mississippi.org

USM Business Assistance Center:
http://www.usm.edu/biac/

Sourcelink Mississippi:
http://www.mybiz.am/

Southern Appalachian Fund:
http://www.southappfund.com

Crudup-Ward Women's Business Center:
http://www.crudupwardactivitycenter.org/womens-business-center.html

MACE Women's Business Center:
http://www.deltamace.org/programs/womens-business-center/

■ MISSOURI

Missouri SBTDC:
http://www.missouribusiness.net/sbtdc/index.asp

Missouri Business Development Program:
http://www.missouribusiness.net

Department of Economic Development:
http://www.ded.mo.gov

Missouri Business Portal:
http://www.business.mo.gov

Chamber of Commerce:
http://www.mochamber.com

Secretary of State:
http://www.sos.mo.gov

Grace Hill Women's Development Center:
http://www.gracehill.org/content/GraceHillWomensBusinessCenter.php

■ MONTANA

Montana Assistance for Veterans:
http://sbdc.mt.gov/2012veterans.mcpx

Montana State Official Business Resource Division:
http://businessresources.mt.gov

Chamber of Commerce:
http://www.montanachamber.com

Montana SBDC:
http://www.sbdc.mt.gov

Montana Business:
http://www.mtbusiness.com

Montana Community Development Corporation:
http://www.mtcdc.org

Secretary of State:
http://www.sos.mt.gov

Montana Women's Business Center:
http://www.prosperabusiness network.org/Default2.aspx?ID=58

NEBRASKA

Secretary of State:
http://www.sos.ne.gov

Chamber of Commerce:
http://www.nechamber.com

Nebraska Business Development Center:
http://www.nbdc.unomaha.edu

One-Stop Business Registration Information:
https://www.nebraska.gov/osbr/ index.cgi

Nebraska Enterprise Fund:
http://www.nebbiz.org

Nebraska Business Success:
http://www.nxbizsuccess.com/

Grow Nebraska:
http://www.grownebraska.org

Community Development Resources:
http://cdr-nebraska.org

Department of Economic Development:
http://www.neded.org/

Nebraska Entrepreneur:
http://www.nebraskaentrepreneur. com/

Nebraska Grants:
http://nebraskaccess.ne.gov/ grants.asp

NEVADA

Secretary of State:
http://www.nvsos.gov

Chamber of Commerce:
http://www.lvchamber.com

Nevada Small Business:
http://www.nevadasmallbusiness. com

Office of Economic Development:
http://www.diversifynevada.com/

Center for Entrepreneurship and Technology:
http://www.ncet.org

UNLV Center for Business and Economic Research:
http://business.unlv.edu/?p=404

Nevada Microenterprise Initiative:
http://www.4microbiz.org/

Nevada SBDC:
http://nsbdc.org

REAP Women's Business Center:
http://www.cfra.org/reap/wbc/

Nevada Women's Business Center:
http://www.4microbiz.org/womens-business-center

NEW HAMPSHIRE

Secretary of State:
http://www.sos.nh.gov

Chamber of Commerce:
http://www.concordnhchamber.com/

Division of Economic Development:
http://www.nheconomy.com/

New Hampshire SBDC:
http://www.nhsbdc.org/

Community Development Finance Authority:
http://www.nhcdfa.org

New Hampshire Business Finance Authority:
http://www.nhbfa.com

Southern New Hampshire University Inc.:
http://www.snhu.edu

■ NEW JERSEY

New Jersey SBDC:
http://www.njsbdc.com

State of New Jersey Business Portal:
http://www.state.nj.us/nj business/

New Jersey Business Center:
http://www.nj.com/business/

Enterprise Development Center at New Jersey Institute of Technology:
http://www.njit-edc.org/

Institute for Entrepreneurial Leadership:
http://www.ifelnj.org

New Jersey Department of Labor and Workforce Development:
http://lwd.state.nj.us/labor/employer/busres/BusinessResources.html

NJ Chamber of Commerce:
http://www.njchamber.com

Secretary of State:
http://nj.gov/state/

Women's Center for Entrepreneurship Corp.:
http://www.njawbo.org/

■ NEW MEXICO

Secretary of State:
http://www.sos.state.nm.us

Chamber of Commerce:
http://www.abqchamber.com

NM Business Resource Center:
http://www.brc.nm.org

NM Economic Development Department:
http://www.gonm.biz/

Association of Commerce and Industry:
http://aci-nm.org/

New Mexico Entrepreneur Alliance:
http://nme-alliance.ning.com/

Department of Veterans' Services:
http://www.dvs.state.nm.us/vetpro.html

ACCION Start-Up:
http://www.accionnm.org/

New Mexico Community Capital:
http://www.nmccap.org

Wesst Enterprise Center:
http://www.wesst.org/

Finance NM:
http://www.financenewmexico.org

Santa Fe Business Incubator:
http://www.sfbi.net

WESST Corp.:
http://www.wesst.org

■ NEW YORK

New York State SBDC:
http://www.nyssbdc.org/services/veterans/veterans.html

Empire State Development:
http://www.esd.ny.gov/small
business.html

New York State Department:
http://www.dos.state.ny.us/

New York State Department of Taxes:
http://www.tax.ny.gov/

New York Chamber of Commerce:
http://www.ny-chamber.com/

New York State Veterans Business Outreach Center Program:
http://www.nyvetbiz.com/

Bronx Women's Business Resource Center:
http://www.bronxwbc.org

BOC Women's Business Center:
http://www.bocnet.org/boc/boc_
services_womens_business_ctr.asp

Women's Business Center:
http://www.ldceny.org/index.asp

Canisius College Women's Business Center:
http://www.canisius.edu/wbc

Queens Women's Business Center:
http://www.queensny.org/qedc/
business/programs/wbc/

Women's Entrepreneurial Business Center, ComLinks Inc.:
http://www.comlinkscaa.org

WISE Center, Syracuse University:
http://www.wisecenter.org

Women's Business Center of New York State, The Business Training Institute Inc.:
http://www.nywbc.org

Women's Enterprise Development Center Inc.:
http://www.wedcbiz.org

■ NORTH CAROLINA

North Carolina Small Business & Technology Development Center:
http://www.sbtdc.org

North Carolina Department of Commerce:
http://www.nccommerce.com/en

N.C. Rural Economic Development Center:
http://www.ncruralcenter.org/

List of Small Business Incubators in North Carolina:
http://www.gaebler.com/North-Caro
lina-small-business-incubators.htm

Secretary of State:
http://www.secretary.state.nc.us/
corporations/

Mountain BizWorks Inc.:
http://www.mountainbizworks.org

Women's Business Center of North Carolina:
http://www.ncimed.com/wbc

Women's Business Center of Fayetteville:
http://www.ncceed.org/help/womens-
business-center/

■ NORTH DAKOTA

Secretary of State:
http://www.nd.gov/sos

Chamber of Commerce:
http://www.ndchamber.com

North Dakota SBDC:
http://www.ndsbdc.org

NDSU Business Support:
http://www.ag.ndsu.edu/small business

Center for Technology and Business:
http://www.trainingnd.com

Disadvantaged Business Enterprise Program:
http://www.dot.nd.gov/divisions/civilrights/dbeprogram.htm

North Dakota Rural Development Council:
http://www.ndrdc.org

ND Maximizing Enterprise Performance:
http://www.ndmep.com

Economic Development and Business homepage:
http://www.business.nd.gov/

OHIO

Ohio.Gov Department of Development:
http://www.development.ohio.gov/entrepreneurship/sbdc.htm

Ohio Small Business Development Centers:
http://www.entrepreneurohio.org/

Ohio Business Resources:
http://www.ohiomeansbusiness.com/

Great Lakes Innovation and Development Center:
http://www.glideit.org/

Ohio University Innovation Center:
http://www.ohio.edu/research/innovation/

The Entrepreneurs Center:
http://www.tecdayton.com

Youngstown Business Incubator:
http://www.ybi.org

Akron Global Business Accelerator:
http://www.akronaccelerator.com

Secretary of State:
http://www.sos.state.oh.us

Chamber of Commerce:
http://www.ohiochamber.com

Alex Community Development Corporation:
http://www.alexcdc.com

OKLAHOMA

Chamber of Commerce:
http://www.okstatechamber.com

Secretary of State:
http://www.sos.ok.gov

Oklahoma SBDC:
http://www.osbdc.org

Department of Commerce:
http://www.okcommerce.gov/

Innovation to Enterprise:
http://www.i2e.org

Grow in OKC:
http://www.growinokc.com

Rural Enterprises of Oklahoma:
http://www.ruralenterprises.com

Oklahoma Capital Investment Board:
http://www.ocib.org

Center for Advancement of Science and Technology:
http://www.ok.gov/ocast/

CHAPTER 5

■ OREGON

Chamber of Commerce:
http://www.oregonstatechamber.org

Secretary of State:
www.sos.state.or.us

Oregon SBDC Networks:
http://www.bizcenter.org

Oregon Innovation Center:
http://www.innovationcenter.org

Business in Oregon:
http://www.oregon4biz.com

Business Development Department:
http://www.oregon.gov/OBDD/index.shtml

COCC Business, Employee, & Professional Development:
http://noncredit.cocc.edu/Small+Business/default.aspx

Small Business Advisory Council:
http://www.sbacpdx.com

Association of Minority Entrepreneurs:
http://oame.org

Portland Development Commission:
http://www.pdc.us

PSU Business Outreach Program:
http://www.pdx.edu/sba/business-outreach-program

The Women's Business Center at Mercy Corps:
http://www.mercycorpsnw.org/what-we-do/womens-business-center/

■ PENNSYLVANIA

Pennsylvania SBDA:
http://www.pasbdc.org/

Pennsylvania Open for Business:
http://www.paopen4business.state.pa.us/portal/server.pt/community/pa_open_for_business/7176

Bridgeworks Enterprise Center Business Incubation Center:
http://www.thebridgeworks.com/

Carbondale Technology Transfer Center:
http://www.4cttc.org/

Industrial Development Center:
http://www.centrecountyidc.org/

Department of State:
http://www.dos.state.pa.us

Chamber of Commerce:
http://www.pachamber.org

E-Magnify, Seton Hill University:
http://www.e-magnify.com

The Women's Business Center at Community First Fund:
http://www.commfirstfund.org/womens-business-center

Empowerment Group Inc.:
http://www.empowerment-group.org

Women's Business Development Center:
http://www.womensbdc.org

■ RHODE ISLAND

Secretary of State:
http://sos.ri.gov/

Chamber of Commerce:
http://www.provchamber.com

Rhode Island SBDC:
http://www.risbdc.org

Urban Ventures:
http://www.urbanventuresri.org

RI Economic Development
Corporation:
http://www.riedc.com

Small Business Recovery:
http://www.rismallbusiness
recovery.com/

BetaSpring Startup:
http://www.betaspring.com/

Brown Forum for Enterprise:
http://www.brownenterpriseforum.org

Business Innovation Factory:
http://www.businessinnovation
factory.com/

RI Nexus:
http://rinexus.com/

Slater Technology Fund:
http://www.slaterfund.com

Center for Women & Enterprise:
http://www.cweonline.org

■ SOUTH CAROLINA

SC Small Business Chamber of
Commerce:
http://www.scsbc.org

South Carolina Business
One-Stop:
http://www.scbos.sc.gov

South Carolina Department
of Health and Environmental
Control:
http://www.scdhec.gov/environ
ment/admin/sbeap/

University of South Carolina
SBDC:
http://www.usca.edu/sbdc/

Secretary of State:
http://www.scsos.com/

■ SOUTH DAKOTA

Secretary of State:
http://www.scsos.gov

Chamber of Commerce:
http://www.sdchamber.biz

U South Dakota SBDC:
http://www.usd.edu/sbdc

SD Enterprise Institute:
http://www.sdei.org

SD Technology Business Center:
http://www.sdtbc.com

Governor's Office of Economic
Development:
http://www.sdreadytowork.com

Small Business Innovation
Research:
http://www.sbir.dsu.edu/

SD Center for Enterprise
Opportunity:
http://www.bhsu.edu/Default.
aspx?alias=www.bhsu.edu/sdceo

South Dakota Community
Foundation:
http://www.sdcommunity
foundation.org

South Dakota Center for
Enterprise Opportunity, Black
Hills State University:
http://www.bhsu.edu/sdceo

▣ TENNESSEE

Secretary of State:
http://www.tn.gov/sos/

Chamber of Commerce:
http://www.tnchamber.org

Tennessee SBDC:
http://www.tsbdc.org

Nashville Business Incubator:
http://www.nbiconline.com

Tech 20/20:
http://www.tech2020.org

Emerge Memphis:
http://www.emergememphis.org

University of Tennessee Center for Industrial Services:
https://cis.tennessee.edu/

Tennessee Valley Authority Economic Development:
http://www.tvaed.com

East Tennessee Economic Development Agency:
http://www.eteda.org

Small Business Guide:
http://www.tn.gov/ecd/bero/pdf/
SGB_smart_guide2011.pdf

Renaissance Business Center:
http://www.cityofmemphis.org/
framework.aspx?page=446

BrightBridge Women's Business Center:
http://www.sewbc.org

▣ TEXAS

San Antonio Small Business Development Center:
http://www.sasbdc.org

Business Start-Up Information:
http://www.sos.state.tx.us/corp/re
lated.shtml

Texas Business Advisor:
http://www.window.state.tx.us/tba/

Entrepreneurial Development Center:
http://www.servicesca.org/

Austin Chamber of Commerce:
http://www.austinchamber.com

Texas Secretary of State:
http://www.sos.state.tx.us/

Central Texas Business Resource Center:
http://www.centexbrc.org/

Small Business Development Program:
http://www.austintexas.gov/depart-
ment/small-business-development-
program

Women's Business Center: BIGAustin (Business Invest in Growth Austin):
http://www.bigaustin.org/?page_
id=71

Women's Business Center: Southwest Community Investment Corp.:
http://www.wbc-rgv.org

Women's Business Border Center:
http://www.womenbordercenter.
com

Women's Business Enterprise Alliance:
http://www.wbea-texas.org

Acción Texas Inc. Business Center:
http://www.stwbc.com

■ UTAH

Secretary of State:
http://www.utah.gov/government/secretary-of-state.html

Chamber of Commerce:
http://www.utahstatechamber.org

Utah Business Incubator:
http://www.utahbusinessincubator.org/

Miller Business Innovation Center:
http://www.mbrcslcc.com/mbic

Utah SBDC:
http://www.utahsbdc.org

Utah Small Business Coalition:
http://www.utahsmallbiz.com

Office of Economic Development:
http://business.utah.gov/

Utah Business:
http://www.utahbusiness.com

Salt Lake Chamber Utah's Business Leader:
http://www.slchamber.com/section/list/view/womens_business_center

■ VERMONT

Vermont SBDC:
http://www.vtsbdc.org/

Agency of Commerce & Community Development:
http://www.dca.state.vt.us/

Vermont Procurement Technical Assistance Center:
http://www.vermontbidsystem.com/

Department of Banking, Insurance, Securities, and Healthcare:
http://www.bishca.state.vt.us/

Vermont Business Center @ UVM:
http://www.uvm.edu/vbc/

Department of Economic Development:
http://www.thinkvermont.com/

Vermont Employee Ownership Center:
http://www.veoc.org/

Chamber of Commerce:
http://www.vtchamber.com

Secretary of State:
http://www.sec.state.vt.us

Vermont Women's Business Center:
http://www.vwbc.org

■ VIRGINIA

Virginia DBA:
http://www.dba.virginia.gov/

Virginia SBDC:
http://www.virginiasbdc.org

Virginia Small Business Assistance Program:
http://www.deq.virginia.gov/Programs/Air/SmallBusinessAssistance.aspx

Virginia Highlands Small Business Incubator:
http://www.vhsbi.com/

Women's Business Center of Northern Virginia:
http://www.wbcnova.org/

Chamber of Commerce:
http://www.vachamber.com

Secretary of State:
http://www.commonwealth.virginia.gov

New Visions New Ventures:
http://www.nvnv.org

Women's Business Center of Northern Virginia:
http://www.cbponline.org/content/view/15/93/

■ WASHINGTON

Washington SBDC:
http://www.wsbdc.org/

Start or Run Your Business in Washington:
http://www.lni.wa.gov/Main/RunBusiness.asp

State of Washington Business Licensing Service:
http://bls.dor.wa.gov/start business.aspx

Chamber of Commerce:
http://www.wcce.org

Secretary of State:
http://www.sos.wa.gov

Starting a Business:
http://www.choosewashington.com/business/start/Pages/default.aspx

Access Washington:
http://access.wa.gov/business/

Department of Commerce:
http://www.commerce.wa.gov

Washington Women's Business Center:
http://www.nwwbc.seattleccd.com

■ WEST VIRGINIA

Chamber of Commerce:
http://www.wvchamber.com

Secretary of State:
http://www.wvsos.com

West Virginia SBDC:
https://www.sbdcwv.org/

Business for West Virginia:
https://www.business4wv.com/

West Virginia Department of Commerce:
http://www.wvcommerce.org

WV Business:
http://www.wv.gov/business/Pages/WVBusiness.aspx

Women's Business & Training Center:
http://www.westvirginiawbc.org

■ WISCONSIN

Chamber of Commerce:
http://www.wisconsinchamberfoundation.org

Secretary of State:
http://www.sos.state.wi.us

Wisconsin SBDC:
http://www.wisconsinsbdc.org

Wisconsin Department of Commerce Business Development:
http://commerce.wi.gov/BD/

Women's Business Initiative Corporation:
http://www.wwbic.com

Forward Wisconsin:
http://forwardwi.org/

U Wisconsin International Business Resource Center:
http://www.uwplatt.edu/ibrc/

Build Your Business:
http://www.wisconsin.gov/state/
byb/agencies.html

**Economic Development
Corporation:**
http://www.wedc.org

Venture Center:
http://www.venturecenterwi.biz/

**Wisconsin Business Incubation
Association:**
http://www.wbiastate.org/

**Western Dairyland Women's
Business Center:**
http://www.successfulbusiness.org

**Wisconsin Women's Business
Initiative Corp.:**
http://www.wwbic.com

WYOMING

Secretary of State:
http://soswy.state.wy.us/

Chamber of Commerce:
http://www.wyomingchambers.com

**Wyoming Technology Business
Center:**
http://www.uwyo.edu/wtbc/

Wyoming Business Council:
http://www.wyomingbusiness.org/

Wyoming Entrepreneur SBDC:
http://wyen.biz/

Economic Development Center:
http://www.wyomingeda.org/

**Wyoming Women's Business
Center:**
http://www.wyomingwomen.org

CHAPTER 5

Bibliography

■ CHAPTER 1

Barringer, B.R., & Ireland, R.D. (2008). *Entrepreneurship - Successfully launching new ventures* (2nd ed.). Upper Saddle River, New Jersey: Prentice Hall.

Birley, S., & Muzyka, D. (2000). *Mastering Entrepreneurship.* Edinburgh Gate, Harlow: Pearson Education Limited.

Boyett, J. H., & Boyett J. T. (2000). *The Guru Guide to Entrepreneurship.* Hoboken, NJ: John Wiley & Sons.

Christensen, C. M. (1997). *The Innovator's Dilemma.* Cambridge, MA: Harvard Business School Press.

Drucker, P. F. (2002). *Discipline of Innovation.* Harvard Business Review, 80(8), 95-103.

Katz, J.A., & Green, R.P. (2009). *Entrepreneurial Small Business.* New York, NY: McGraw-Hill.

Office of Veterans Affairs and U.S. Small Business Administration. (1985). *Entrepreneurial Veterans: Examination and Comparison.* Retrieved from http://archive.sba.gov/advo/research/rs70v2.pdf

Pew Research Center. (2000). *The Military-Civilian Gap: War and Sacrifice in the Post-9/11 Era.* Retrieved from http://www.pewsocialtrends.org/files/2011/10/veterans-report.pdf

Society for Human Resource Management. (2010). *Employing Military Personnel and Recruiting Veterans.* Retrieved from http://www.shrm.org/Research/SurveyFindings/Documents/10-0531%20Military%20Program%20Report_FNL.pdf

United States Small Business Administration. (2012). *Veteran-owned Businesses and their Owners - Data from the Census Bureau's Survey of Business Owners.* Retrieved from http://www.sba.gov/sites/default/files/393tot.pdf

Veterans Have Entrepreneurial Spirit, Study Shows. (2005, February). *Franchising World, 37(2),* 94-95.

Waldman Associates. (2004). *Entrepreneurship and Business Ownership in the Veteran Population.* Retrieved from http://www.sba.gov/advo/research/rs242tot.pdf

CHAPTER 2

Boughton, L., & Dyer, P. (2011). Victory: 7 *Entrepreneur Success Strategies for Veterans.* Newport Beach, California: Bandera Publishing.

CHAPTER 3

Ardichvili, A., Cardozo, R., & Ray, S. (2003). A theory of entrepreneurial opportunity identification and development. *Journal of Business Venturing,* 18, 105 – 123.

Barringer, B.R., & Ireland, R.D. (2008). *Entrepreneurship - Successfully launching new ventures* (2nd ed.). Upper Saddle River, New Jersey: Prentice Hall.

Birley, S., & Muzyka, D. (2000). *Mastering Entrepreneurship.* Edinburgh Gate, Harlow: Pearson Education Limited.

Copeland, M. V., & Malik, O. (2006, June 1). How to Build a Bulletproof Startup. *Business 2.0 Magazine,* 7 (5).

Drucker, Peter F. (2002). Discipline of Innovation. *Harvard Business Review,* 80(8), 95-103.

Eckhardt, J.T., & Shane, S.A. (2003). Opportunities and entrepreneurship. *Journal of Management,* 29 (3), 339 – 349.

Green, R., & Carroll, J. J (2000). *Investigating Entrepreneurial Opportunities.* Thousand Oaks, CA: Sage.

Hess, E.D., & Goetz, C.F. (2009). *So, You Want to Start a Business? 8 Steps to take Before Making the Leap.* Upper Saddle River, NJ: FT Press.

Katz, J.A., & Green, R.P. (2009). *Entrepreneurial Small Business.* New York, NY: McGraw-Hill.

Ryan, J.D., & Hiduke, G.P. (2008). *Small Business: An Entrepreneur's Business Plan* (8th ed.). Mason, OH: South-Western Cengage Learning

Sutton, R.I., & Pfeffer, J. (1999). *The Knowing-Doing Gap: How Smart Companies Turn Knowledge into Action.* Cambridge, MA: Harvard Business School Press.

▨ CHAPTER 4

Barringer, B.R., & Ireland, R.D. (2008). *Entrepreneurship - Successfully launching new ventures* (2nd ed.). Upper Saddle River, New Jersey: Prentice Hall.

Birley, S., & Muzyka, D. (2000). *Mastering Entrepreneurship.* Edinburgh Gate, Harlow: Pearson Education Limited.

Katz, J.A., & Green, R.P. (2009). *Entrepreneurial Small Business.* New York, NY: McGraw-Hill.

Meyer, M.H., & Crane, F.G. (2011). *Entrepreneurship: An Innovator's Guide to Startups and Corporate Ventures.* Thousand Oaks, CA: Sage.

Moorman, J. W., & Halloran, J. W. (2005). *Successful business planning for entrepreneurs* (1st ed.). Cincinnati, OH: South-Western Educational Pub

Ryan, J.D., & Hiduke, G.P. (2009). *Small Business: An Entrepreneur's Plan* (8th ed.). Mason, OH: South-Western Cengage Learning